YOU
MAKE THE
DIFFERENCE

THE FINANCIAL ADVISORS PERFORMANCE GUIDE TO MARKETING YOU!

YOU
MAKE THE
DIFFERENCE

THE FINANCIAL ADVISORS PERFORMANCE GUIDE TO MARKETING YOU!

Stan Hustad

Kirk House Publishers

Minneapolis, Minnesota

You Make the Difference
The Financial Advisors Performance Guide to Marketing You!

Given the legal environment, we suggest that you consult your compliance or legal advisors in adopting the ideas presented in this book. We have not intentionally included any advice or materials that put you at risk, but we also realize how quickly and often laws and regulations change regarding the financial services industry

This publication is designed to provide accurate and authoritative information in regard to the subject matter covered. It is sold with the understanding that neither the author nor the publisher is engaged in rendering legal, accounting, or other professional service. If such assistance is required, seek the services of a licensed professional.

PTM
G R O U P

10	9	8	7	6	5	4	3	2	1

Library of Congress Cataloging-in-Publication Data
Hustad, Stan P., 1945
  You Make the Difference: The Financial Advisors Performance
    Guide to Marketing You! / by Stan P. Hustad
    p. cm.
  ISBN 1-886513-42-2 (alk. paper)
  1. Personal Development. 2. Financial Planners. 3. Self help. I. Title

Kirk House Publishers, PO Box 309459, Minneapolis, MN 55439
www.kirkhouse.com

Manufactured in the United States of America

In a good business book . . .

The writing should be clear and understandable, the ideas thoughtful and practical, and the written text easy to see and read.

The visual design of this book is different than most. It is specially designed by Wendy Johnson of Points Of View Incorporated/EE Design located in Minneapolis, MN. The ideas and principles used in the text and page design make for greater clarity with the goal of achieving an ease of reading.

To find out more about these principles, contact Points Of View/EE Design at www.pointsofviewinc.com or 800-586-9054.

Thanks...

To Karen who makes the good life possible for me.

To Amy and Megan for wise counsel on thinking and writing clearly.

To many friends and clients who have trusted, encouraged, and supported me in my life and work.

Contents

Foreword by Joe Pine – Co-author of *The Experience Economy* 1

Introduction To Personal Performance Marketing –
This Is For You! 5

Chapter 1
Fear Kills Everything 11

Chapter 2
Image Is Not Everything,
But It Is The First Thing 29

Chapter 3
What Do You Really Want? 45

Chapter 4
Turning Your Mission Statement Into
Greater Commission Statements 55

Chapter 5
Do You Believe? 75

Chapter 6
You Have One Minute To Tell Your Story 85

Chapter 7
The Future Belongs To The Storyteller 103

INTERMISSION 117

Chapter 8
    Don't Be Afraid – You Can Give A Talk! 121

Chapter 9
    The Tape's Rolling – Be A Personal Performance
    Broadcaster To Your Clients And Prospects 129

Chapter 10
    It's Your Turn In Your Town,
    And You're On Stage 147

Chapter 11
    Be A Writer And A Powerful Marketer 157

Chapter 12
    You Are The Brochure When You
    Tell Your Story 173

Chapter 13
    I Am Grateful When You Recommend Me
    To Others 189

Chapter 14
    The Marketing Rule of Seven Changes
    Everything 207

Chapter 15
    Break A Leg: A Challenge And A Benediction 221

Performance Notes 229

Foreword

by Joe Pine
co-author of *The Experience Economy*

When asked to think about how financial advisors should market themselves, I'm immediately reminded of the 1970s M*A*S*H episode where one of the U.S. soldiers recuperating under Hawkeye's care is a life insurance agent in civilian life. Despite his involvement in fighting the war in Korea and a newly broken arm, this guy keeps hawking insurance. He never stops selling, selling, selling. The doctors, the nurses, his fellow patients—they all sooner or later find themselves trapped in a metaphorical corner with a guy who won't take "No" for an answer. I can still remember his signature line: "People don't plan to fail; they fail to plan!"

Sure, some of his prospects actually buy—but, as I remember it, mostly just to get rid of the guy. When it comes time to renew, forget it; this guy will be long gone. He's only after one-time commissions. He will not make a difference in his clients' lives.

And it shows in his sales technique. He's always smiling the same plastic smile; he doesn't listen, for his mouth is always moving, using the same lines no matter the prospect's situation; and his hand is always reaching for that pen in his attempt to close the sale. In short, he's plastic—a fake, a phony, inauthentic.

Man, does that guy need this book. (Well, *if* he were real—which he wasn't—and *if* he were still in the business— which he wouldn't be—*then* he would really, really need this book.) And so do you. No, I'm not saying you're as bad as that guy—indeed, given your desire to improve your performance (else you wouldn't be reading this), you're probably already a pretty good financial advisor. But you can be better, and Stan Hustad is just the man to help you. (And if you happen to be reading this but are *not* in the financial industry, two words: Keep reading. Almost everything Stan says here applies to any professional industry involving one-on-one selling and performance.)

Based on the wealth of his background and the depth of his work in coaching executives throughout the financial industry, Stan provides an abundance of ideas and practices that you can immediately put to use to improve your marketing capabilities, generate new business, and enhance the connections you make with clients, because in the end you will learn to deserve that business. Every single chapter contains a gem or two (or three). Just a few samples:

- **Create not only an image, but become a person of grace and good manners.** (What an amazing little piece of advice—and how very needed today.)

- **Be you, only more so.** (Amen.)

- **It's not about traditional prospecting; it is about attracting.** (Simple and effective: don't target customers, but become so attractive that they target you.)

- **Who are you?** (It doesn't get more real than that.)

In many ways, *You Make the Difference* particularizes to the financial industry what my partner, Jim Gilmore, and I wrote in *The Experience Economy: Work Is Theatre & Every Business a Stage.* We showed that, in the face of goods and services everywhere being commoditized, what customers want today are experiences that engage them in an inherently personal way. And when staging such an experience, work is theatre, and therefore—as a financial advisor—your performance is your offering.

Note that this is not a metaphor (not work as theatre) but a model: whenever you are in front of a potential or current client, you are acting. Whether you know it or not; whether you do it well or not; you are acting and need to do so in a way that engages that audience in front of you. This doesn't mean you become fake or phony—that's play-acting—but rather you make real choices about how you present yourself—your real self—in front of your clients.

Stan independently developed his own ideas on performance through his background as a professional communicator and dramatist (which meld perfectly with our's). He cogently reveals those ideas in this book, providing commendable, practical, doable (not to mention eminently readable) advice for how exactly to *perform* on the bare stage of business. And he applies them in particular to *your* world, your business, your exact needs as a financial advisor. To ignore what Stan has to say is to imperil your ability to succeed in the emerging Experience Economy.

Let me close as I began, with another anecdote from the 1970s. This one's not fictional though; it comes from real life—my life. In high school, my favorite teacher taught philosophy and also coached the chess team. He wasn't a particularly good chess player—every one of us on the team could beat him—but he was a pretty darn good coach. (I especially liked his move my senior year, consenting to my request to be moved from chair 1 to chair 2 so I could actually win a few games against, alas, rather formidable competition.)

And this guy was an even better philosophy teacher. For our final assignment in that class, we each had to write down our worldview, which were all published together in a single volume for the whole senior class to read. He challenged us to think, truly think, about what we believed and why it mattered. He made us face our post-high-school future, examine our path, and put a stake in the ground to mark where we stood. He forced us to write our thoughts down in a logical manner, so that anyone could understand how we viewed the world and our role in it.

I don't know about the rest of the kids in the class, but this assignment made a huge impression on me. It made me reflect (what did I believe?), it made me resolve (yes, this is it), and it made me bold (to share my freshly solidified world view). I still have that collection of papers to this very day.

That teacher is still playing much the same role today, for it was Stan Hustad. He made a difference in my life and, through this book, he can make a difference in yours.

Dellwood, Minnesota
January, 2002

Joe Pine, co-founder
Strategic Horizons LLP

Introduction to
Personal Performance Marketing

THIS IS FOR YOU!

It is a phrase that people love to hear. One of my careers was as a broadcaster with an international radio station on the little island of Bonaire in the southern Caribbean. Our late night music, news, and musings program was called "Caribbean Night Call;" and it attracted a large audience. I would often get musical requests from our listeners, and I would honor those requests by giving the title of the song, the name of the person making the request, and then say, "this is for you!" The audience loved that. More and more, I have learned the power of those simple words. All of us want, even love to know that we are noticed, that we are special, that we are of consequence.

Today, one of the major trends in business models and marketing practices is called One-to-One Marketing. This idea rejects so-called mass marketing as obsolete and less and less effective. We are challenged by the one-to-one marketing thinkers to seek deeper knowledge and understanding of our clients and customers, so that we can market our goods, services, and experiences to their specific desires and preferences. However, one-to-one marketing communication is not a new idea to the broadcasting professional. I often coached my younger broadcasting colleagues to seek to speak to "one person" as they produced their programs, and to think of the one listener they were trying to connect with on each particular program. I told them that if they tried to reach everybody with everything, they would probably reach nobody with anything. The paradox of broadcast communication is that when you powerfully focus your message for a few, you often reach many more than you intended to.

Effective communication and marketing is inherently personal. Marketing communication is me speaking to you and saying, "this is for you." As a producer and announcer, I was marketing both my message and myself. The listener had to experience the feeling that she was the very special person that I was talking to. It was personal marketing—but it was more. In the best sense it was always a performance and I always had to be "on" for my audience. I marketed my message, my services, and myself by performing as host, speaker, friend, and trusted confidante.

That is what this book is all about. It is about **personal performance marketing** of your financial advising services. Personal performance marketing is demonstrating that you possess warmth, wisdom, expertise, and can provide the experience the potential client needs to fulfill their hopes, dreams, and solve their problems. To work with the people you want, you will have to market yourself so they will know you, notice you, and be attracted to the professional financial services you perform. In the twenty-first century you will not be able to effectively market yourself by phone calls, sending letters, or conventional advertising. You will have to do it by performing in a way that attracts prospects and clients. From now on, do not talk about prospecting, think about attracting.

So if you are interested in being a performance marketer, this book might be for you. But there is more to think about. This book is based on the idea that you must be the difference. Many financial service advisors advertise their products, their services, their company, and the brands that they represent. I not only suggest a different course of action, but difference in a greater sense. There is to be something about what you believe, and how you perform that cannot be duplicated. This book will challenge you to perform at your best, and to know how to promote the unique you to the unique person you seek to serve and influence. Tom Peters, business writer and guru has written in **The Brand You 50: Or: Fifty Ways to Transform Yourself from an "Employee" into a Brand That Shouts Distinction, Commitment, and Passion!**[1] that there are ways to shout your difference and sell, sell, sell. I think differently. This is not a book to help you shout or spin and create a fast in your face sales image. It asks you to be different in your service and in your marketing efforts. It asks you to develop a marketing image that includes deep integrity. It asks you to believe that if you become a better person and a better advisor, people will come to you and your business. If you are looking for hotshot sales ideas, ways to get the customer, their money, and move on, then this book is not for you. It is not about old hard nose traditional selling ideas, data base management, mailing lists, letter writing, and drafting brochures. If you seek that kind of technical detail, others can help you. Personal performance

> *"This book will challenge you to perform at your best, and to know how to promote the unique you to the unique person you seek to serve and influence."*

marketing is about becoming a person who believes that we have only one entitlement in life, and that is to create value for others.

A final note. In another part of my career, I was a school-teacher. I taught a course in high school on the world's great philosophers and thinkers. One of the ways that I performed for my students was to sing, albeit poorly, a little rhyme that went something like this:

This is the way the world is,
This is the way it makes sense—
This is the way the world is,
This is the way we try to make it make sense.

Ultimately, this was what the thinkers we were studying were offering. They helped us to know what makes sense about our world, other people, their behavior, and ones self. To be a good marketer, you need to be a bit of a philosopher. You are trying to understand the human condition, motivation, and the situation that we are in. I have found that the best financial service advisors are men and women of professional expertise and wide interests. They know their field, and they also have a deep-seated intellectual curiosity. Their bookshelves contain more than financial, business, and marketing books. They read widely in fiction, psychology, religion, philosophy, drama, and even children's literature. They, to use an old-fashioned phrase, are truly renaissance men and women.

Brian Tracy, a premier human potential and achievement thinker, has said that one of the best keys to success is thoughtfulness.[2] He means that we should think often about our life goals and what is important and valuable to us. I agree that we should be thoughtful, and with a double meaning. What we think about we become; and what we think about, we tend to do. But being thoughtful also means being mindful of others. Success is grounded in the ability to treat every person you meet as if they were the most important person in the whole world. That is thoughtfulness in action, and it will help you in becoming a great marketer—and even more important, a person of great value.

I often say the essence of good marketing is to help the people who should say no to a product and service to say so. So if I have done this right, you may know that this book is not for you. But if what I have said makes sense to your head, rings in your heart, and makes you want to enjoy marketing your financial advising services, then this book is for you.

Chapter 1
FEAR K<small>ILLS</small>
EVERYTHING

"Remember, that whatever you dread, fear, you are attracting, because the mind always relates with whatever dominates the thought. That which we think about most we get, and it is the easiest thing in the world to kill the possibility of realizing our ambitions and drawing to us the thing we fear by holding it in mind, by allowing doubt thoughts, anxious discouraged thoughts, to get possession of us and strangle our efficiency."   – Orison Swett Marden

"The history of the human race is the history of ordinary people who have overcome their fears and accomplished extraordinary things."   – Brian Tracy

"We do not have the spirit of fear but of power, love, and self-confidence."   – Saint Paul

It was a family reunion to honor an aunt and uncle who were celebrating their Fiftieth wedding anniversary. Their children and grandchildren were there along with a host of other friends and relatives. While we were eating the hors d'oeuvres around the punch bowl the conversation turned to what was new in our lives since we had last been together. One of the guests stopped the conversation by announcing that he had left his company and was starting a new business venture on his own. This drew attention because most of the listeners knew that he had a very good job as a sales representative for a major company. He was good at his work, had a top-notch income and a lifestyle to match. We wondered, how he could just leave that income and security. He explained the new venture he had in mind, and showed real enthusiasm for the steps he was taking for the new business. The growing audience expressed their admiration, but also expressed the fear they would feel if they were taking such a risk. After a long pause, the new venturist said, **"Don't you know you can't go down that way of thinking ... don't you know that fear kills everything?"**

Indeed it does, Fear kills hopes, aspirations, and dreams. It kills relationships, confidence, and creativity. It can kill our joy and rob us of happiness. It can even ruin our health and take our life. "Scared to death" is not just a figure of speech, for some it is a reality. My punch bowl philosopher friend had revealed a great truth—don't you know, fear kills everything?

If you want to have a successful business as a professional financial advisor you must deal with the cold grip of fear. You may have bought this book hoping that you can market yourself and your practice better, make more money, and not have to be so afraid. Some of you have picked up this book as a final attempt to make your practice work. You are hoping that you might find a formula to rapidly increase your business success, increase your income, and diminish your fears.

Most of you do not feel that desperate but you may feel a little bit inept when it comes to marketing. You may be a good well-informed advisor with all of the right information and latest technology. But that is not enough today. That leads back to the subject of fear and a fundamental truth. **Marketing your services, your wisdom, and your professional expertise has many challenges; but the first and continuing challenge to marketing yourself and building your financial advising practice begins with overcoming your fears.** The less fear you have, the more successful you will be. Personal performance marketing begins by understanding the fears that steal your confidence and creativity, and knowing how to overcome them. There are five fears that can stifle your success in building and marketing your financial services practice. They are powerful, but if understood, can be overcome.

"The less fear you have, the more successful you will be."

The five fears we face are:

1. The fear of failure and poverty.
2. The fear of rejection.
3. The fear of offensive selling.
4. The fear of having nothing important to say.
5. The fear of believing that we have no value.

The fear of failure and poverty

The most profound fear that you will face as an entrepreneurial financial advisor in marketing and building your practice is the fear of going broke. Poverty is frightening. One client told me about once seeing a large cardboard box and how that image stayed with him and frightened him in the early days of his venture. He had visions of himself as homeless and living in such a box. It was intensely visual and very gripping to him. The fear of losing your livelihood, of not being able to pay the rent, buy food, can be as intense as the fear of losing your life. The fear of poverty is primal; it is a deep part of the human situation. Don't feel ashamed or inferior because others can handle this fear better than you can. People handle this deep fear differently based on their personality, temperament, experience, and faith. Many motivational speakers have stories of people who felt this fear and then just went out and made it happen. They tell how these brave people overcame their fear and became successful. There are many stories like that. But the other side of the stories are often not so bright. There are true stories of many others who were overcome by panic, gave in to depression, and failed in their attempt to market themselves and build their professional service or their enterprise. These equally true stories are usually not included in those "you-can-do-it" speeches. The good feelings and courage that come from the Friday motivational speech soon fade in the hard and fast reality of a Monday morning full of rejection and anxious anticipation.

Every person must devise their own strategy for creatively dealing with their fear of failure and poverty. But if the fear of failure and poverty is profound in your life you will find personal performance marketing very difficult. A successful marketing strategy takes time, creativity, and a sense of self-confidence. When you are afraid that you are going to lose it all, it is very hard to take the time necessary to do well and be patient for the results. Your heightened anxiety may lead you to action, but it is often

"A successful marketing strategy takes time, creativity, and a sense of self-confidence."

desperate action and not creative marketing activity. The fear of failure and poverty might motivate you to go out and sell something (a policy, annuity, or some other product). But that is selling, it is not marketing. Such desperation selling can even work against you. People who are seeking professional help with their financial situation are not attracted to people who are desperate for business. If you appear greedy, needy, or desperate, you will not be attractive.

Fear will be with you as long as you seek to live any kind of independent entrepreneurial life and work style; and that is what you are if you are a financial advisor. But if your fear becomes pervasive, it will affect your performance so much that a time-out might be in order. You may need time to recoup your courage, resources, and remind yourself of your talent. That does not make you a failure. The world is full of successful people who had to do other things as they built their business or their professional practice. A very successful literary agent tells of driving a taxi to make ends meet and using the colorful cast of characters he met in his cab as subjects in essays to increase his own writing skills. An investment banker tells of delivering the Wall Street Journal in the early mornings as a way of supplementing his income as he built his own investment venture.

I have worked with people who built their financial advising practices, and marketed themselves well, using what I call the "slide approach." They did a slide, gradually and incrementally, from one line of work into their successful practice. While keeping another source of income going, they patiently, creatively, but with great certainty, began to define their business (the primary part of marketing), provide services to new clients, and market themselves. They also continued to enhance their reputation and build their professional network until one day they found themselves with clients, confidence, and the courage to now "go for it all." This is a sound strategy, and you might consider it if you are dealing with the fear of failure and poverty. It is okay to take a break and restore your confidence and creativity, to find ways, however temporary, to make the income you need. Use your "day job" as a way to learn. This will give you time to become good at what you do, and do a good job of marketing. But good marketing takes time. So be bold, be brave, but don't be stupid if you are in the grips of the fear of failure and poverty.

The fear of rejection

The second fear you may face as you market yourself and your advisory services is not as gripping as the fear of failure and poverty. But it may keep you from reaching out to others in your marketplace. It is the fear of rejection by others. For most of us, this is a big problem. Few of us have masochistic tendencies; no one wants to be embarrassed. Rejection and refusals are not only uncomfortable, they hurt. There are hundreds of books on sales and marketing, and every one of them talks about the fear of rejection. In some cases, the advice is very simple, and a bit stoic. We are told to "get on with it, get over it, don't take it personally," and just remember "for every 'no' you hear, you are one step closer to hearing a 'yes'." We are told that sales is a numbers game, and you just have to go through those rejections until you come up to someone who wishes to do business with you. There is some truth in these ideas. The call to be courageous, step up to what is uncomfortable, make a presentation, and move on if they say "no," is commendable. Learning how to come back from rejection and disappointment is vital to true success. But any coaching and advice that says about your fear of rejection, "get used to it, grow up, and keep going," is too simplistic. As a professional financial services advisor you are not offering a product like heavy equipment, or a service like carpet cleaning, that people simply do or do not want or need at the present time. You are offering yourself as well as your services, and despite all of the mental toughness you seek to muster, it is hard not to take it personally.

> *"It is also important to know that your personality type and past experiences can play a part in how you deal with the big fear of rejection."*

It is also important to know that your personality type and past experiences can play a part in how you deal with the big fear of rejection. Some people can maintain great personal boundaries between their professional life and their personal psyche; others cannot. Some people have very strong egos, which allow them to take rejection and not be troubled. Others are not that strong. I have even discovered that some very strong sales-people types have sociopath tendencies. They have no real feelings or empathy for others and, in a corollary of that, have no concerns about the feelings and perceptions of others. They don't mind rejection, because they simply do not care what the other person thinks or feels. Fortunately, these people are a small minority. For many of us life has had many rejections; and then to go out and get more rejections in the sales and marketing game may be too much to handle. The problem is that many people who have difficulty in handling rejections, may possess exceptional skills, wisdom, and experience, which may be lost to us all, not because they can't perform their services, but because they fear the rejection that's part of the sales and marketing experience.

Perhaps you are stifled by the fear of rejection. The performance marketing approach, which is ultimately about attracting clients and prospects, in order to build a financial advising business is helpful to those who have a strong fear of rejection. The performance marketing approach does not seek to cajole or overcome people's objections as much as it seeks to find ways to connect with and convince people to consider you as their professional advisor.

The performance marketing approach can also lead you to a whole new view of "rejections." As strange as it seems, to a good marketer, rejections can be a positive. If you want to be successful in your financial advising practice you

> *"As strange as it seems, to a good marketer, rejections can be a positive."*

will be continually refining your preferred client profile. You will know which people are the best personal and professional fit for your services. So if a person is not in the preferred profile, they may reject your offer, and you might in turn reject them as people who cannot be best served by you. In this case rejection becomes selection, and choosing, and that is what the marketing approach seeks to have people do. It helps people make good choices.

This leads to another possible positive when you adopt a marketing mindset. What happens is what I call a "mental mind jump" that can transform the view you have of yourself and your business. You start seeing yourself as a selector of qualified prospects and clients rather than begging for whoever will do business with you. When you know that your message, value, and values are clear and communicated well, and your worth not in question; you gain that mental power that allows you to say that the listener (prospect) is either not ready yet or not a good fit. When you have a marketing view of your advising practice, you understand that either you or the prospect can reject the other, because rejection has now become a matter of mutual selection. The fear of rejection is gone, and when that happens you are on the verge of a significant and profound breakthrough in your performance and in the results you will achieve.

The fear of offensive selling

The title may tell the tale. High on my bookshelf, I see the title of a book similar to this one. It is entitled **Marketing Your Services For People Who Hate To Sell.**[1] In another very good book, there is a chapter entitled, "Honk if You Hate Marketing." If the authors of these books are correct, and understand the marketplace and the human condition, then many professional service providers must hate selling and marketing. Financial service advisors are different from professional service providers such as consultants, dentists, chiropractors, and accountants who also have to sell their services. Those people went into their professions, and perhaps not have fully understood all the implications. Most financial advisors, on the other hand, enter their career knowing full well that sales and marketing is a vital part of their required performance. Still, the vast majority of financial advisors leave the business within three years. This is usually not because they were unable to perform the professional financial services, but because the marketing and sales part became an insurmountable challenge. So it is very possible that you along with many other financial service advisors also hate the sales and marketing part, and that you dislike being "just another (<u>insert your least favorite expletive or description</u>) salesperson." Let's meet this fear and overcome it.

You may also find selling and self-promotion to be very uncomfortable and unnatural, and you don't want to do that. You may find such behavior embarrassing. From your own experience, you know how you react to the person who is continually selling, marketing, and self-promoting. You know that you don't want to become that kind of person. You don't want to live a life where you are continually trying to overcome objections, and persuade people to do something they do not want to do. Everyone has been in "sales situations" where they have found the hard sell approach objectionable and distasteful. When you are put into that kind of a sales situation, you hate to be there. So perhaps you are afraid that if you have to get involved in selling and marketing that you literally might have to do and become what you hate. These, and for many other reasons, are all a part of why you and many other advisors may be stifled by the fear of offending.

Personal performance marketing, however, is not connected to the stereotypical salesperson image. The Willie Loman character portrayed in Arthur Miller's ***Death Of A Salesman***[2] is dead in professional circles. Yes, there are a number of relics from that not-too-distant past still loose on the economic landscape, but their days are numbered. Modern consultative selling is much different. Look at it this way. When you go to the doctor you are going in for a consultation. Most of us do not object when the physician, upon hearing our complaints, begins to ask us questions about our health, our symptoms, and our present situation. Upon hearing those complaints, she suggests certain activities and perhaps writes us a prescription. In effect, as a result of her consultation, the doctor is asking us to go to the pharmacist and buy drugs and medication. Few of us object to that; in fact, we welcome it. Now, you don't have to follow through and go to the pharmacist. You are at choice. You can choose to accept or reject your physician's recommendation. Your physician may warn you of the consequences if you don't follow through and participate, but you have a choice. At its very best, consultative selling is very much like what you receive in a professional medical consultation by the most professional practitioner. When selling is seen that way, it is different.

Years ago, Peter Drucker, management consultant, pointed out that when marketing is done well, selling would take care of itself.[3] Even though he made the statement in the 1950's, it is still a source of controversy within sales and marketing circles. But go to the meaning that Drucker put to his observation, and it makes profound sense. For Drucker, "marketing" is understanding the client or customer needs and wants, and envisioning solutions that would make their life and work better. With this understanding in place, the marketer knows that when a clear presentation is made and performance demonstrated, the customers can discover the value themselves. Then they can easily and confidently make their decision and their selection. In Drucker's thinking, if the marketing is done well, the prospect is the one who closes the sale; they sell themselves. To some, this describes

". . . if the marketing is done well, the prospect is the one who closes the sale . . ."

almost a utopian vision of the marketing process. They will point out that it can never go quite that way. Perhaps they are right, but unless you aspire to such a vision of how you can market yourself and your services, you will not be able to achieve it.

Personal performance marketing is based on the premise that when you demonstrate your professional expertise and wisdom with energy, enthusiasm, and great skill, you will attract potential clients and customers into your circle of influence. While these people are under your influence, they will increasingly see the value, select you as an advisor and make professional recommendations to people in their centers of influence. It can happen, does happen, is happening to many of your colleagues, and it can happen for you. So put away your fear of selling.

The fear of having nothing important to say

Years ago, William Shakespeare said that all the world was a stage and each of us has many parts to play. Many years later, in the 1950s, Erving Goffman wrote a very influential book entitled *The Presentation Of Self In Everyday Life.*[4] In this classic work, Goffman showed how each person plays dramatic roles in how they present themselves socially in all their relationships, and professionally in the way they do their work. Recently, Joe Pine and Jim Gilmore have taken the model even further. In their book entitled, *The Experience Economy, Work is Theatre & Every Business a Stage,*[5] they describe how the present economic environment has moved from products and services being what we offer to clients and prospects, to a marketplace that requires us to also provide "experiences" for them. They claim that almost all products and services have been reduced to being commodities. That means that there is no substantial difference between the products and services being offered at competitive levels. Pine and Gilmore then assert that if we want to have a competitive edge we must create experiences that people find delightful, of value, and increase their choices and sense of personal significance. Fundamental to their analysis is their prescription that in order to create experiences of value, we must understand that our work is theatre and our business a stage.

> "... in order to create experiences of value, we must understand that our work is theatre and our business a stage."

Pine and Gilmore's analysis, along with the insights of Goffman and the wisdom of Shakespeare, can help you as a financial advisor in two distinct but related ways. Most financial advisors have fallen into the dilemma that Pine and Gilmore describe—they have become mere sellers of policies, funds, and plans. Those are now commodities that can be bought and sold by anybody in anyplace. These advisors have nothing unique to offer and no compelling experience or added value that makes their work or their service unique. Because of that they have nothing to say when they approach potential clients. They sense it and in some case know it, and that is why they are afraid—they fear that they will be rejected, neglected, and discounted because they have nothing new to say.

But there is more, and this is part of personal performance marketing. Since we all are on stage in the experience economy, we need to give increased attention to how we speak our parts to the audience (clients and prospects) that we seek to attract and influence. But at this time most financial advisors have had no training or coaching in speaking their parts. They have no strong scripts that describe their work and what they are really good at. They have not had help in learning how to use the phone, the mass media, how to give a group presentation, or to truly know their roles and how they can best play their parts and speak their lines.

Let me assure you that if this describes you, you are not alone. The vast majority of financial services advisors often find themselves at a loss in knowing how to describe themselves and how to answer the simple question, "What do you do?" Many of you do not feel confident in describing the work you do and how you are unique and different in your performance. But like every good actor/performer, you need to know your part. You need to know the right cues, and you need to know what to say. You need to know how to ask questions in a way that is compelling, inviting, and attracting. You also need to describe the work you do in ways that causes people to ask you questions, and you need to reach people at deeper levels of their experience. Much of what personal performance marketing is all about is getting better at what you do, and then knowing what to say, how to say it, and when to say it so you can attract and influence the clients and prospects you want to select you as their financial advisor. But until that time, many of you will still be

"Much of what personal perform-ance marketing is all about is getting better at what you do, and then knowing what to say, how to say it, and when to say it so you can attract and influence the clients and prospects you want to select you as their financial advisor."

fearful of having nothing to say. But with time, hard work and good coaching, things do not have to stay that way.

I challenge you to take Pine and Gilmore's dramatic model very seriously. Start thinking this way. You have to be "on" and perform for your audience—clients and prospects. You must find ways to attract that audience, delight them, sometimes even entertain them, creating memories for them, and communicating in engaging ways that motivate them to work with you. From now on, remember this program is a performance guide to viewing your work as theatre, your business as a stage, and the role you play as central to your success. But also remember that "performing" does not mean faking, play acting, or pretending. In fact, just the opposite is true. You'll be called to perform with purpose, power, poise, clarity, self-assurance, and a heart for service, because that's what you are becoming and who you are.

The fear that we have no value

The final fear that can stifle our success and steal our joy is related to the fear of "having nothing to say." Many people don't know what to say, because they have nothing to say. Sometimes we may look at the work we do and how we do it, and realize that we simply may be providing what everybody else provides. There may be no extraordinary or even unusual value in who we are, what we do, and in how we do the things that we do. The expression "value added" has become a part of modern business. We are continually challenged by the question, "and what value do you add?" People can buy insurance and financial services over the Internet, with no commission added to the asking price.

Well-educated people will ask the question, "If I pay you a commission, what value did you add?" Hundreds, perhaps hundreds of thousands of jobs have been lost and will continue to be lost because people who were doing those jobs did not add any value. The work they were doing and the processes they were providing have been replicated, duplicated, mechanized or provided by somebody or something else. Remember, unless you provide some added value or experience, you not only have nothing to say, indeed, you have nothing to offer. That is a fearful place to be.

> *"Remember, unless you provide some added value or experience, you not only have nothing to say, indeed, you have nothing to offer."*

One of the primary premises of personal performance marketing and coaching programs is that you must bring yourself to a level of service and creativity where you do bring extra value and a unique experience to your clients and prospects. But just as important as providing it, you need to know what to say and how to demonstrate your value in ways that delight the client and prospect, making their life easier and more enjoyable. When you do this, it will go well for you and you will not be afraid of having no value.

. . . Some final thoughts on fear

Fear does kill everything. If you are seeking to market yourself and your financial services business, you must understand these fears and how you can begin to deal with them. Perhaps you can even overcome them. Keep in mind that even the boldest and the bravest will never fully overcome their fears. But you can have less fear, and greater courage and self-confidence. The writer Parker Palmer, in talking about leadership in our world today, suggests that we will always have some fears and some great anxieties in our life. But in a line that touches me deeply with it's truth he says, **"but we don't have to become our fears."**[6] Yes, fear does kill everything. But we have within our power and within our faith, the ability to not be afraid.

Chapter 2

Image Is NOT EVERYTHING But It IS The FIRST Thing

"Facts as facts do not always create a spirit of reality."
– G. K. Chesterton

"Know first who you are and then dress accordingly."
– Epictetus

"A man's style is his mind's voice."   – Ralph Waldo Emerson

Image is everything. That's the motto, even "the mantra" of many marketers in fashion, music, sports, entertainment, and even in politics today. Savvy marketers tell us that the investment in creating "the image" is the key to entrepreneurial and professional success. There are many strategies, stories, and successes that sustain that belief. But for you as a financial services advisor there is a small but profound difference. The truth is, **image is *not* everything, but it is the *first* thing.**

Let me explain. There are a variety of ways to define and describe an "image." I use the following definition of "image" in personal performance marketing.

"Image is a vivid description, a representation, a personification of our poise, performance, and the experience that we can provide that is projected to others. Images are created to influence people in positive and powerful ways.

Let's examine how this works. Image is the vivid and powerful way you represent who you are (personification) and what you do (your service performance and the experience you bring) to the people you seek to influence so you can attract clients and customers, and then serve them well. *When you seek to market your professional services, you must first deal with the image you want to project.* The reason you must do this is that we live in a very image conscious and media saturated culture. Television and video have not only shaped our culture, but according to some researchers they may have even "rewired" our brains. Today, people buy and vote by the sound bite and graphic image. Constant information and image overload have reduced their attention span. The smart marketer knows that they may only get one opportunity to connect with a prospective customer or client, and that opportunity may be only a few seconds long.

Unfortunately, because of this, your first encounter with potential clients is seldom one where you can communicate real integrity and substance. Today you often must begin with image and style. It may not be fair, but often we have to begin our relationship with potential clients based on a vivid projection of a promise to perform in a way that is different, delightful, and memorable. That is a part of having an image; and it is the first thing you need to do if you want to market yourself and your business.

Today we live in a culture where "spin" is in and where the "sizzle" may be sold as more important than the steak. However, I reject these cultural and marketing standards both personally and professionally. *I believe that character is better than cute; substance is more important than style; education is preferable to mere entertainment; and integrity must be behind and supportive of any image.* So as you create your image, make sure that it is truthful as well as attractive, confident as well as humble, exudes kindness to others, and reflects well on you and what you do. Any business or professional service based only on image will eventually fail. It's only a matter of time. With this understanding at the heart of all you do, let's seek to better understand why one still needs to give careful and continued attention to image as the first thing.

The problem of invisibility

Years ago Ralph Ellison wrote a classic story about race relations in America in the novel *Invisible Man.*[1] It was a story of how ignored and invisible a young black man felt as he sought to make his mark in the world. Few of us today can compare our plight with that of a poor young black man trying to make it in the early 1950s. But the title is helpful. In your attempt to better build your business as a financial services advisor, you are essentially invisible. Derek Lee Armstrong and Kam Wai Yu, in their book, *The Persona Principle, How to Succeed in Business With Image Marketing*[2] stated the problem profoundly and simply: "The biggest obstacle to your success is invisibility. The best, the most experienced, and the most talented people cannot enjoy prosperity until they are visible to their potential market."

As a professional financial advisor you have to deal with this issue from many sides. First of all, many financial services are intangible. As a financial advisor, you are marketing and selling products that can't be held, seen, smelled, or experienced directly. Next, the best prospects for your services may also be invisible in terms of need, desire, or opportunity. Every autumn a gentlemen comes to my neighborhood and knocks on my door and offers to sell me a cord of firewood. His job is easy when it comes to identifying prospects. In our area, homes that have fireplaces can be easily identified by chimney design. He simply goes down the streets, identifies those homes, and offers his firewood. Unfortunately many of the people that you seek to serve as a financial advisor are not so easily identified. Their need and readiness are not immediately visible. Finally, and most significantly, you yourself are invisible. The people who might need you and the services you provide probably don't know that you exist, what you do, or how it can help them. Invisible, invisible, invisible—this is the challenge that creating an image as the first thing will help you overcome.

Overcoming invisibility

Creating your image is just one of the ways to overcome the problems of invisibility. But there are other ways. First, you can get a break. You can be in the right place at the right time. You can be there when people are looking for your services, and you just happen to be available. Not only are you available, but the influence you gain from the service that you provided leads to other significant contacts and recommendations.

Unfortunately, these situations are not nearly as common as we would like to believe. Most likely, what appear to be lucky breaks for some people are really the result of long and hard work. I recall an actor who said that his seemingly overnight success and fame due to his appearance on a successful TV sitcom, was "an overnight success that took over twenty years of hard work." Don't count on the breaks.

Next you can spend money, often significant amounts of money, to have your services proclaimed and published in public places and spaces. This is advertising. Tons of paper is consumed and hundreds of hours of airtime are bought every day so companies and their products can be seen by others. They want to lose their invisibility. The problem with advertising as a way of enhancing your visibility is that it can be very expensive, and any eventual success may not match your costs in time, money, and energy.

Third, you can scream and shout. "Scream and shout" is industry slang for public relations. Public relations is seeking creative ways to advertise with greater

". . . you can scream and shout."

subtlety and sophistication. It has the advantage over advertising in that it seeks to build relationships, create positive experiences, demonstrate expertise, and places your name and services in front of significant audiences. It can be very effective, and it can also be very costly. Public relations might be one of the ways that you make yourself more visible. However, it works best if you first have an image to show to the public.

Finally, you can be very present, very persistent, and perhaps even be a pest. This is simply sales activity. The premise of what we call traditional selling is the proverbial numbers game. The premise of all such selling is that if you jump in front of enough people and keep doing it, your persistent presence, or maybe just your plain pestering, will yield some results. Continued selling activity will allow you to reduce your invisibility and enhance your public profile.

All of these are ways of dealing with your invisibility. But creating a simple, unique, and distinct image may be the most effective and inexpensive way to be seen. If you do decide to use any of the other ways of being visible, they will be more effective if you do them with your image in mind. So once again, image should be the first thing.

You already have one

Another reason why creating an image should be the first thing is that you already have one. One of the fundamental principals of communication theory is that you "cannot not communicate." This means that everyone is always communicating something. It may not be what you want to convey, but your presence, body language, words or non-words all say something. The same thing is true of you and your professional services. Your profession as an advisor already has an image in the eyes of many people.

Let me demonstrate. When you see or hear the words "lawyer, CPA, dentist, minister, insurance agent, auto salesmen, consultant, banker, or writer," many emotions, prejudices, and images come to mind. These are all based on your past experiences and your present perceptions. The image that you have of these professions impact any contact that you may have with any of these people. The same is true for you. One of the reasons you need to do your image work first is to play on the positive images that people already have of you or your profession, or to differentiate yourself from the images people have that are negative or mundane. One of the fundamental principles of marketing is, seek to be different from the competition. Show the difference and the uniqueness that you possess. Since your profession has an image of some kind, the first thing you need to do is create an image that highlights you and your unique abilities.

Image is an inexpensive way to start.

The third reason why you should do your image first is because it is one of the least expensive things you can do as part of a personal performance marketing program. A now legendary story in marketing tells how the famous Nike image of the "swoosh," was created by a design student for just a few dollars. What Nike got in that simple image creation is probably similar to the legend of acquiring Manhattan Island for twenty-four dollars. The story demonstrates that a simple attractive image need not be a costly venture. Of course, good design is of great value, and good graphic design can be expensive. But part of the genius of good image work is that you can have high impact with minimal investment.

"... part of the genius of good image work is that you can have high impact with minimal investment."

Image—the most important thing

The final reason why image is the first thing is that it helps you do the most important thing—that is, "be the client, think like the client, and serve the needs of the client." It is very easy to get caught up in the enthusiasm for the work that you do, the service you provide, and the hopes you have for making a difference for others. But the best thing you can do in creating your business and marketing approach is to literally see it as the client would see it. When you create an image, you must decide who the prospective client is and what it is they want. You will have to try and figure out what will grab their attention, keep them interested, and find ways to demonstrate your expertise; and then to influence them to seek your professional services. Image creation is communication to the client, and by giving it a strong priority in the work you do, you begin to think less of yourself and more about the clients whom you hope to have an impact on.

In my experience, I have found that many financial advisors still lack the empathy and the ability to put themselves fully in the place of a client. When you create an image, knowing that it is to be seen and perceived by the client, you are doing the key work of identifying the people in your market, the services and the experiences that you will provide, and the positive results people can enjoy because they work with you. If you do not take image creation seriously, you are not taking your marketing seriously.

"If you do not take image creation seriously, you are not taking your marketing seriously."

How you can begin

Creating an image is not an easy project. You will benefit by getting a coach or an advisor with strong communications, performance, and mass media experience to help you. It is deeply personal work. As you work through this book, as you define your market, interests, expertise, and the stories and values that shape you and your practice, ideas will come to you. You will begin to seek and receive advice and wisdom in these three image areas:

- Your personal communication, leadership style, and care for others.

- Your personal presence, poise, appearance and attractiveness to others.

- Your printed material including business cards, stationery, and brochures.

But to get you started let me suggest some practices and principles that you can consider and use to enhance your personal style and your professional image. One of the best ways to build your image is to gain a reputation, not just for your persona and fine appearance, but the poise, graciousness, and good manners you possess. The following are some suggestions to help you create not only an image, but become a person of grace and good manners.

1. **Do what you say you will do.** This is very simple and perhaps it seems too obvious. However, it is one of the best things you can do, and it is one of the rarer qualities found in the business world today. When you make a promise, keep it. When you say you will do something by a certain time, have it done by that time or get back to the person with an explanation

and re-open the negotiation. Make this part of your image building vital to all that you do. Whenever you say you will do something, make sure you do it.

2. **Be very present.** Personal presence is one of the most powerful ways of building your image and increasing your influence. As one coach said in advising his financial service clients, "Be prepared to show up and be no place else." You can have incredible influence and power by being totally focused on the person that you are working with, helping, and listening to. Our industry has too many people who talk about themselves, are always looking around, interrupting others with their own opinions and seek to be the center of attention. You may want to get coaching to help you develop this powerful personal quality. If you view every social encounter as an opportunity to be fully present and fully aware of the other person, you will be known for the quality of your listening and the quality of your performance.

3. **Always say "thank you."** A number of years ago, Robert Fulgham[3] suggested that most of the things necessary for personal and professional success were learned in kindergarten. I would say, *should have been learned* in kindergarten. I'm often surprised by how many people still do not know how to say "please" and "thank you." When someone does something for them, they forget to say "thank you." When someone has helped them or recommended them, they forget to write a thank you note. Be different and remember that to live well and be successful today you need to have an attitude of

ongoing gratitude. Be grateful to God for the gift of life and prosperity. Be grateful to others for their sustaining care and concern for you. Be grateful to clients who by their patronage of your service and their recommending you to others are vital to your success. Always say thank you.

4. **Apologize when you are wrong and even when you're not.** Gain a reputation for never blaming others or defending yourself. If a mistake was made, apologize, say you're sorry, and ask for forgiveness. Make every assurance that you can that the mistake will not be repeated. If someone else makes a mistake, do not blame them or seek to find a way to place blame. Nothing positive is achieved because somebody was able to push the blame to somebody else. What difference does it make in future success? When you have the humility to admit when you are wrong, say you are sorry and ask for forgiveness, you will increasingly find that people are attracted to you by the poise that you show and the kindness that you share.

5. **Stand up and greet people by their name.** It may sound a bit old fashioned today, but I suggest that it is even more relevant today. When you are at a table or a desk, and someone comes to you, stand up and greet them. Use their name whenever you can. Now don't get me wrong. The excessive use of a person's name is an old salesperson's trick, and such sophistry and sham behavior can easily be spotted. I'm simply suggesting that when you know a person's name that you demonstrate the importance of their name and

show the importance of their person by your manner of greeting them. In Asian societies, a simple bow acknowledges to the other that a source and spark of divinity is to be found in the other. When you stand for another person, you simply assert that no matter what, you find dignity in the person you are meeting. So whenever it is appropriate, learn to use a person's name as you stand up.

6. **Don't interrupt.** We see it and hear it, and perhaps suffer through it all the time. One person is asking a question or making a statement and another cuts them off quickly, or worse, interrupts them. Don't interrupt others. Cultivate a habit of the "pregnant pause." After a person has finished their statement or asked a question, give a pause to think, to reflect, to show respect and then make your point. This does not mean that you have to accept everything they say, or that you believe every proposition that they make. It simply allows civility to come back to your conversation, gives a sense of peace and quiet (which we all need in our social interactions), and allows you the full power of making an uninterrupted statement yourself. A reputation for pausing, and then speaking, will profoundly enhance your personal communication image.

7. **Give simple gifts.** Gain a reputation for giving simple gifts. In your business and in your personal and professional life, learn the art of the simple gift. When a client has done business with you or recommended you to others, it is appropriate to find a suitable simple gift that says, "I value your

recommendation, and thank you." It should not say too little (all those trinkets and trash with advertising slogans), nor should it say too much, as if some reciprocation and more recommendations are to be expected. It simply says the right stuff. Gain the grace of giving simple gifts.

8. **Give away your stuff.** This is a corollary to our past recommendation but it goes further and has even greater implications. The so-called "New Economy" changes many things in the marketing equations. One of the things that is increasingly true about the "New Economy" is that we can gain power and influence by not hoarding all of the things we have. Our influence will grow and our image will be enhanced when we are not so protective of our possessions, talents, and information. One very successful author has given people the choice of buying his book or downloading the whole thing from the Internet. Many others will follow him. These writers know that by showing an attitude that lacks greed, lacks fear, and demonstrates an ability to share, that in the end they will be far better off both in reputation and in revenue. So as you cultivate your image, find ways for you to give away your "good stuff."

9. **Treat others as the most important people in the world.** It is incredibly powerful and simple as it can be. Earl Nightingale, one of the foremost thinkers in the area of personal and professional success, said many years ago, that the key to success is "to treat every person as if they were the most important person in the world."[4] Think how much better you

would feel and how much better it would go for you if you would do this. The stories of salespeople and others who have lost millions of dollars in sales because they treated secretaries and assistants as second-class citizens are legion. It is vital that you gain a reputation of treating other people as if they were the most important person in the world. We do this because they truly are.

10. **Be you, only more so.** One of the problems is that people are learning all kinds of image enhancing and success strategies that teach you to fool other people into believing that you are more than you are. Unfortunately some people, rather than trying to be better at what they do, try to cover up who they are with a mask of exaggerated importance. They are more "ego" than value or experience. Take the time with a coach, or someone who cares deeply for you, to do the work of discovering who you really are. What is the role that you are called to play in the drama of life? What are the secrets of your personal success and your own performance that reside powerfully and deeply within you? You are not here to try to be something you are not. You are not here to cover up your weaknesses. You are here to perform at your best, develop your strengths, and find others to help you with the things that you cannot do. Nothing will put a person more at ease than to find a person who is confident in who they are, creating value based on who they are, and careful to include others in any project of significance and success.

Remember, who you are and how you care for others will ultimately be the key to the image that follows you as a financial services advisor. Now that you have the image and style idea in hand, let's make sure that you are becoming the person who is attractive because you know what you want out of life. That's next.

Chapter 3

What Do **You** Want?

"Our wants serve us almost as well as our possessions."

– Jen Guehenno

"It's funny about life, if you refuse to accept anything but the very best, you often get it." – Somerset Maughan

"There is only one quality more important than 'know how.' This is 'know what.' By which we determine not only how to accomplish our purposes, but what our purposes are to be." – Norbert Wiener

Personal performance marketing as a way of building your financial services advisory business is based on a number of beliefs. A fundamental one is that you, the advisor, not any company or broker-dealer, or any of the vast array of products, funds, or portfolios, or even the technology that you possess, are the reason why a client chooses you to be their advisor. It is your wisdom, your expertise, your attention, your service, your kindness, and the enjoyment they find in working with you that makes the difference. It's your personal performance that drives your business and your marketing.

Next, personal performance marketing is based on a belief in the power of attraction. The power of attraction is not just some philosophical idea. It is a reality confirmed by many successful and influential people. I often state this belief by paraphrasing the expression that came out of the film, "Field of Dreams." In this story about building a baseball field in the middle of a cornfield in Iowa, the main character was told by "the voice" that "If you build it, they will come." In the financial services business, one could say "if you become, they will come." Personal performance marketing is not about traditional prospecting; it is about attracting.

"You will attract people who are like you."

This leads to a third and vital belief. You will attract people who are like you. Your clients are a very good reflection of you and your performance. The kind of person you are will be the kind of clients you get. So this marketing business is not just about how you perform and what you do. In a deeper sense, it is about the kind of person you are. Let me ask you this question. Would you like clients who are successful, influential, goal directed, creative, decisive, courageous and with a bias towards action? The answer is obvious. Well, if you seek clients like that, then you need to be or become like that.

Let me give you an example. As a favor to a client I called on a colleague to suggest that he join us at an introductory coaching workshop for only fifty dollars. He didn't know if he wanted to do that. He could not make that decision and take that risk. In our meeting he told me that part of the problem was, "clients these days." He had just received a phone call in which a client could not make a decision to purchase a simple fifty thousand dollar term life insurance policy. I left his office after he declined my offer and I wonder if he ever figured it out. He has clients just like him.

This story can be repeated time and time again. If you want to attract the "quality folks" to your business, you are going to have to do the work of becoming a person of "quality," of "influence," of "true success." You are going to have to be one of those rare persons who truly thinks about their life, their goals, their money, and the things that they want to achieve. You must know what you want! That's where we need to do some work. Knowing what you want serves to help motivate you as you build your business and design the life you wish to lead. It also helps you to become the kind of person you would want to have for a client.

What do you want?

What do you want? It is a simple question and yet some of the brightest people cannot answer it. When I work with a client seeking to improve their life and business, I always ask, "what do you want?" Once we get beyond some of the trivial and obvious things, such as more money, happiness, and some adult toys, most people are stuck. The sad fact is that most people do not have any real idea about their hopes, desires, wishes, and goals for a good life. When pressed, most people confess that almost all of their energy goes into what I call "DWD" activity. They are fortunate if they can just **"Deal with the Day."** I don't stand in judgment of this. Sometimes dealing with the day is a major accomplishment in itself. But if you are seeking to live the life of a successful entrepreneur as a financial advisor, you will have to live differently. You will have to do what successful people do on a regular, even daily basis. You will look at your life and business and decide very specifically what you want.

You will need to grow in your confidence and enhance your creativity so that you can have the poise necessary to go for what you want. You will need to have a plan for focused action. You may need to have a coach to help you follow through and finish what you seek to start.

> *"You will need to grow in your confidence and enhance your creativity so that you can have the poise necessary to go for what you want."*

There are a number of anecdotal studies and related research that indicate that only three to five percent of the population live their lives with a deep sense of vision and purpose, matched with specific goals and a plan of action. A popular speaker and teacher, Earnie Larson, has said that "people with this kind of personal power don't just live differently in degree, but different in kind." They live differently because they live with desire, intensity, and intentionality rather than by default and accidentally. The challenge to you is to seek to become one of these three-percent persons, who lives with purpose, poise, and a plan. Remember, people want to work with people like them or with people they would like to be. One of the best ways to market yourself is to demonstrate by your life and practice that you walk your talk. You talk about hopes, dreams, goals, success, and future plans. Then you walk that talk by living a life where you figure out what you want, and know how to work a plan and achieve your goals by having the courage and confidence to follow through until you get what you want. You then have the right to speak about goal setting and goal achievement. You have no right to be a financial advisor unless you have a sense of what you want and how to achieve it. You can't share what you don't have.

How to become one of the three-percent who know what they want and are working a plan.

Some people come by the focus, the intensity, and the achievement motive to perform at their best and make their mark in a natural way. However, most need some guidance. To be a goal-directed person, you can find a number of books, videos, audio programs, seminars and coaching programs that can help you. But to get you started, please give some thought to these simple but very important questions. They will help you gain a much deeper sense of direction and intention.

The five questions that can focus our thoughts and lead to effective action.

Here are five key questions for reflection and action that can help you come at the big question, "what do you want," from a variety of viewpoints. When you take the time to be thoughtful about these questions, you will be rewarded with increased clarity about your life and business and have greater ability to influence others who seek the same ideal.

1. **How do you want to be remembered?**
   This is one of the classic questions that comes from ancient wisdom. Some believe that Saint Augustine first posed it in the fourth century. It asks us to look at our life and see it in terms of a legacy. In more recent times, Stephen Covey said that one of the habits of highly effective people was that they "begin with the end in mind."[1] This question asks you to do

that with your life. An exercise that I often give clients is to practice writing an old tombstone. In earlier times, the family and friends of the deceased would write a memorial; and this would be engraved on the tombstone. I ask people to decide what they would wish others to say about them after their life has passed. In a similar vein, I often ask them to plan the ideal memorial service that commemorates their life.

Here are the questions we might ask: What would the tributes be about? What music, poems, literature, or words from their holy writings would be presented? All these preferences are a way to help you to create or discover a sense of purpose about your life. Do some of this work and do it in these ways.

- How do you want to be remembered by your friends and family?
- What reputation do you wish for in terms of your character?
- What are the things you want to achieve?

These three things—your vital relationships, the content of your character, and the important achievements—are ways to focus around the question of how do you want to be remembered. It is a good question for you, and it is also a very good question for your clients and prospects. The next question asks you to get even more specific about the life you seek to live.

2. **If you had no limits, what are the things you would like to have, the things you want to do, the kind of person you'd like to be, and who are the people you would really like to help and serve?**

   These questions give you permission to dream and find some of your deep hopes and wishes. They also encourage a priority that will help you be more successful. Having nice things is good; doing things is better. "Becoming as a person" is even greater; and service and concern for others is one of the highest virtues. Take a piece of paper or a notebook and start writing these things down. Then write their importance on a scale or a system that works for you. Give some thought to the time involved. Are these wishes to be fulfilled in the year ahead, or will they take five, ten, twenty, or more years?

   The answers to these simple questions about having, doing, being, and serving should be updated every year. If you do this, it will change your life. The same question posed in a variety of ways can be one of the most powerful ways to ask your clients to give you a sense of their hopes and wishes. Remember, your work as an advisor is not to sell stuff, but to help clients achieve their hopes and dreams. That may make you a hero to them, and that is where we go next.

3. **What do you want to be like when you grow up?**

   Obviously, I am playing with the question, "What do you want to be when you grow up?" This is a legitimate question at almost every age. I have had many

successful people who said they were seeking my
coaching in order to answer that very question.
They were in the process of seeking second careers
or re-inventing themselves. So it is always a good
question, but here we are seeking a slightly different
insight. You become what you think about, who you
admire, and the personal qualities that you value.
Who do you admire and who do you want to be like?
What about their life, character, beliefs, and achievements are meaningful to you. Think about these
people. They can be famous people or largely
unknown. They may be living now or long in the
past. They can be people that you are personally
acquainted with, or someone you know only by their
reputation and influence. For some reason there is
some vital spark about them that draws and attracts
you to them. Give some time to find the model and
life mentors who help you say, "As I grow older, I
would like to be more like _____. " These thoughts
and reflections lead us to a fuller answer to the question "what do you want?"

4. **In three years, where do I want my career and business to be?**
   Long range strategic planning of over five years is
   not very fruitful. We should have a long-term vision
   in view of how we want to be living and working. But
   that goes back to question two about having, doing,
   becoming, and serving. In this question, I simply ask
   you to look at your business three years ahead in
   terms of the market you will be serving, the growth
   you will be experiencing, and the revenue you will

be achieving. In three years where do you want to be? No one can predict the future, but with deep awareness, we can plan to create a part of it. This is not a time for sky blue dreaming. This is a time for realistic goal setting. Look at your business and declare where you want it to be in three years. These goals should be reachable, stretchable, but not requiring a miracle. Once again, just another way to think about, write, and plan for, what do you want.

5. **How do you want your life to be different in six months?**

   This is a very practical and vital way to start to live with a strategic edge. Peter Drucker, the legendary management consultant, in a series of interviews, suggested that today's business organization should take a time-out every six months to re-examine their mission. Is the mission still appropriate, and is the organization fulfilling it? I suggest that all of us do the same kind of work with our lives in all aspects— personal, professional, relational, financial, and spiritual. Looking at a date six months ahead is a very simple exercise. Start to think, list, and decide how you want your life to be different. In the next six months, what should you then start doing? What should you stop doing? What should you complete? What needs to change? What will make you happier? If every other of the five questions has you stalled or in a slump, start with this one. In doing so, you are beginning to answer the question of what it is you want.

There are other questions to consider, but these are the important ones. With these thoughts in mind and captured on paper, you can start to live differently. With a colleague or coach to help you, your goal setting awareness will increase. People will notice, your confidence will increase, and you will find that you can become a model for people who are seeking and striving for success. People who are serious about investing, building wealth, and achieving success are attracted to men and women who know what they want. Marketing your business requires that you be an example of what the client wants to be and achieve.

Remember, insurance, investments, annuities, mutual funds, and financial planning have no ends in themselves. They are merely vehicles to achieve life priorities. When your clients are no longer just concerned with dividends, income projections, and the details of the products, but become emotionally engaged with deep life issues and seeking ways to do the right things to be successful, the products will fall into place with little resistance. By asking clients these same questions you ask yourself, you become a life advisor and a financial consultant. Others are insurance sales people and product peddlers, but you are different. All of this begins to happen when you know what you want and can help others decide what they want. Now that you are becoming the kind of focused, effective person people want for an advisor, you need to get your message out there. That's next.

Chapter 4

Turning Your MISSION Statement Into GREATER COMMISSION Statements

"Sell where you can . . . you are not for all markets."
– Shakespeare

"To boldly go where no one has gone before."
– Mission of the Starship "Enterprise"

I can almost hear it now since I've heard it so many times before in my coaching workshops for financial advisors. Someone says, "the last thing I need to do now is to waste my time with some mission statement stuff. I need practical help to help me build my business . . . market, and make some money." That feeling is very understandable, and it may reflect your experience. I want to help you see it differently.

While there is power in the personal reflection that comes from making a personal and professional mission statement, sometimes those mission statement workshops do seem a bit philosophical and without practical purpose. Here I want you to consider how a mission statement can be very practical by helping you create powerful marketing messages. The mission statement then leads to marketing statements that can help build your business and increase your commission statements. They are the basis for how we will do our marketing and the goal of marketing is to enhance our influence and increase our income. Doing this requires a focus for your business and a real heart for the work that you do. In fact, you must be a missionary with a mission.

You must be a missionary

Earlier in my life I was involved in volunteer missionary work for my religious faith. It is a calling that requires passion, sacrifice, and a desire to serve others. I suggest that financial advisors need to think of themselves as mission-aries with a message for those that they seek to help. Part of this insight comes from a very fine book written over ten years ago by Anthony Putnam entitled *Marketing Your Services— A Step-By-Step Guide for Small Businesses and Professionals.*[1] I am indebted to him for the following clarity, which will help you understand why you need to have a mission. Mr. Putnam tells a wonderful story about what he calls "Zorba the Professional." It is a delightful illus-tration that refers to the old film, "Zorba the Greek." In the film, Zorba is a free spirit who just wonders around doing whatever he wants. While seeking some work the prospective boss said to him, "What work do you do?" Zorba said, "Listen to him! I've got a head, hands, feet—they do their job. Who the hell am I to choose?" Putnam declares that most of us are just like Zorba in that we haven't made a choice as to what we do. This leads Putnam to a demonstration of positions that most service professionals are in. I have slightly modified his position grid to help you understand his and my point. On one part of the grid, you have either a high or low view of your mission. You also have either a high or low place in a profitable market. You are in one of these four quadrants.

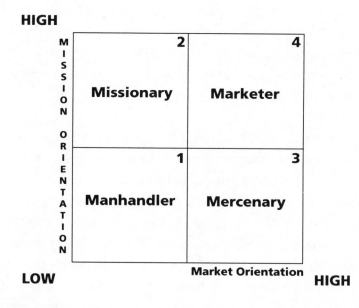

Let's describe each of these situations:

Position No. 1: Low Market, Low Mission—Manhandler
This is my name for what Anthony Putnam called Zorba the Professional Position. These people are just doing whatever they can do to make a living somehow. Like Zorba, they don't choose. I call them "manhandlers"—they just try to get their hands on something, and they try to handle it. There is little

intention or strategic direction in their business. In this position there is no mission and no significant market orienta-
tion toward a significant income. The questions that you
hear most from these kinds of people are:

> *What's hot?*
> *What's working now?*
> *Do you have any good sales ideas?*

They are just trying to find some place where they can make
a buck. I have discovered that many insurance and financial
advisors have a significant relationship to Zorba the
Professional. Often they are merely manhandlers in their life
and business. This is not the way to live well.

Position No. 2: High Mission, Low Market—Missionary

Position No. 2 is a powerful one to be in, but it may not be
very profitable. These advisors are "missionaries" and they
have a cause, a process, and a specialty in which they
believe. They may be very good at performing their services
and delivering expertise, value, and service. The problem is
that they do not have a profitable market to which they can
deliver their services, or if they have one, they haven't figured
out how to reach the people in their market in a consistent
way. They find that their income suffers, not because they
are not focused on their work, but because they don't focus
on how to reach and influence the men and women in the
marketplace. They don't know how to consistently connect
so that the prospects and clients will take action. They are
invisible to the profit point in the marketplace. As a result,
this advisor with a mission often gets distracted and begins
to behave a lot like Zorba. You might be a missionary, and
that's good. But it might not make your business successful.

Position No. 3: High Market, Low Mission—Mercenary

Every profession has people in it who simply go for the money. They have the inclination and perhaps the ability to find and produce revenue. But they are in a constant search for what is working now. They are the ultimate "show me the money" kinds of operators. Mercenary is a negative term, but we do not want to be too harsh. By "mercenary" we mean they have only one ambition and that is to perform for money. They are not concerned with any mission and are only concerned with client satisfaction as it impacts revenue. Mercenaries have to be constantly selling and searching because they have no focus or ongoing market. It's a tough way to work and live, but these people live on adrenaline and go wherever they can and do whatever they have to do to make the money. I remember a typical mercenary who said, "You want pinstripes? We will give you pinstripes." He said this to indicate that he didn't care or have any customer concern or focus. Their attitude is, whatever people say they want, promise them you will get it, and then see if you can. I do not suggest that you adopt the mercenary point of view.

Position No. 4: High Market, High Mission—Marketer

This is where you want to go. Here you are a marketer. This is where your experience, your wisdom, the things you love to do, and the people you seek to work with all come together. The power of your focused mission is leveraged because your efforts are focused towards a specific group of people who understand your mission, can benefit from it, and can pay for the services that you provide. Even better, you are doing this work with people you respect and enjoy. That's the goal of the marketer.

But as Anthony Putnam demonstrates, to be a marketer, you need to be a missionary. If you are a professional advisor, you have to believe in something. You have to want to benefit others and make their life better. You have to enjoy using your wisdom and experience to make a contribution to the life and business of others. But that is not enough. Your missionary spirit must be combined with market savvy, and requires a laser-like focus. As Putnam says, "To become a marketer, first become a missionary. Then find the best possible market for your mission and align yourself with that market." I would add only one thing: it should be the best market for who you are as well as for your mission.

> *"If you are a professional advisor, you have to believe in something."*

This powerful description and position grid by Anthony Putnam is useful in helping you decide where you are and how you can get to position No. 4. Once you get to that position you will have to speak your mission, perform it, and attract people to it. To get there we have to start drafting the mission statement.

Drafting your mission statement

Thinking about a mission statement is a way to answer the simple question: "What do you do?" Think about some of the answers you and others give like, "I'm an insurance agent, I'm a financial planner, I sell mutual funds, I'm a broker, I'm a financial representative." There is nothing wrong with these occupations. For many of you it is not just an occupation, it is a calling. The problem is that they don't really say anything. Just a few examples illustrate this point. Let's start with this one: "I'm an insurance agent." First of all, as discussed in Chapter 2, everyone you meet will bring their own image and definition to this description. But, there are other problems. No one wants insurance. It is a part of life that successful, responsible, and thoughtful people have to deal with, but no one wants insurance as such. It does not strike a powerful, positive, emotional response in the hearts and minds of prospects and clients. I have a client who is very successful as a marketer and an insurance consultant. Yet he often found himself saying to those talkative types on airplanes when he wished to be left alone, "Oh, I'm an insurance agent." That usually worked, he confessed, and the conversation would not go very far.

If you're a marketer, that's exactly the opposite response from what you want from most people. But most importantly, simply saying you're an insurance agent is not saying enough. What kind of insurance, and to what kind of people? Most importantly, it fails to describe what you do to benefit people in specific ways. Here is another example of a statement that does not say enough: "I'm a financial planner." This is better, but there are still problems. Most people will find that vague, and they may not wish to show their ignorance by asking more. It's also possible that clients don't really want a financial plan. What they want are the benefits of a financial plan, such as security, lower tax bills, being out of debt, making money, and many others. That is the problem. You know all the gains that can come from a financial plan, but the answers that you give seldom communicate the value in what you do.

The purpose of a focused and powerful mission statement is to make it possible for you to be prepared to make a variety of marketing statements in any situation. These marketing statements will increase your confidence, describe your services, and lead to greater commission statements.

How to start doing your mission statement

Putting together your mission/marketing statement is hard thoughtful work. I remember a wise coach who once told me that the process can take over a year, and that even then you will need to continue to refine it. At first, I was doubtful. I assumed that a focused hardworking person like me, and others like me, could do it much faster. I soon discovered that one can start and speak your mission much sooner, but my mentor was right. It was well over a year before I really had a strong powerful statement, and I continue to refine it as my business grows and my understanding of my market increases. So be prepared to do what all good and proper things require to be successful. Be prepared to give it some hard work.

Your mission statement should answer four questions for you. Then you can speak the answers to your prospects in precise and powerful ways. The four questions are these:

1. **Who are you?**
2. **What do you do?**
3. **Who do you serve?**
4. **What do you want your clients to feel, experience, and do, because they work with you?**

These questions are in ascending importance; the last one being the most important. Let's briefly describe how these questions work and how they can work for you.

Who are you?

Think about words that describe you as a person who performs for others. Which of these words fit you and your professional practice in a way that you enjoy and embrace? Some of these words we already use; broker, advisor, agent, and planner, are just a few examples. But I would encourage you to look at your life and your practice, and see if you can describe yourself in unique, distinct, and perhaps non-traditional ways. For instance, one of my clients has long been a volunteer ski instructor for various youth programs. He has gained a reputation for being a very fine ski coach.

". . . look at your life and your practice, and see if you can describe yourself in unique, distinct, and perhaps non-traditional ways."

Many of his clients know and appreciate his professional work, and his work as a volunteer. As he looked at his life and the way he both works and would like to work, he said, "I am a coach, always have been." He now describes himself as a financial coach. He reports that this helps define himself and his work in a very positive way. There are other terms that can be used to great effect—such as educator, analyzer, evangelist, preacher, teacher, choreographer, designer, advocate, communicator, counselor, builder, and philosopher. These are all ways that many financial advisors have described themselves and their approach to serving others.

In the following pages, I have provided a long list of descriptive words that end with "er/or." These are words that describe what people do. In some cases I have added just-for-fun words that I have made up. You can probably add words to the list and make up some too. Find seven words that describe you and your work. Then of these seven, choose the top three. From these three, ask yourself if there is one word to which you say, "that's it, that's me, that's who I am at work." This can be a fun and powerful way for you to begin a mission description that refers to you, your story, your style, and the way you do your work. Think about it and come up with some words that suit you, and, most importantly, help your listener understand that you are not just like all the others. Find words that demonstrate that you are different.

Which of these words describe you?

Actor	Brother	Commentator
Advocator	Builder	Communicator
Adventurer	Buyer	Competitor
Advisor		Composer
Ambassador	Caller	Conductor
Analyzer	Calculator	Confronter
Announcer	Caregiver	Connector
Arranger	Caretaker	Conqueror
Assister	Carpenter	Cooker
Auditor	Cashier	Coordinator
Author	Catalyzer	Contributor
	Catcher	Counselor
Baker	Challenger	Counter
Banker	Character	Creator
Bargainer	Cheerleader	Crusader
Befriender	Chooser	Customer
Beginner	Choreographer	Customizer
Believer	Classifier	
Bookkeeper	Cleaner	Dancer
Bridger	Coacher	Dealer
Broadcaster	Collector	Defender
Broker	Comforter	Designer

Describer
Developer
Differentiater
Diner
Discipler
Discoverer
Director
Dispatcher
Doctor
Dreamer
Driver
Drummer

Educator
Empowerer
Encourager
Energizer
Engager
Engineer
Enlightener
Entertainer
Entrepreneur
Examiner
Exciter
Executor
Expediter
Experimenter
Explainer
Explorer
Extractor

Facilitator
Farmer
Father
Fighter
Financier
Finisher

Fire Fighter
Fisher
Fixer
Flyer
Focuser
Follower
Forgiver
Founder

Gardener
Gatherer
Giver
Goal Setter
Go-Getter
Grace-Giver
Grandfather
Grandmother
Greeter
Grower
Guider

Harnesser
Healer
Helper
Hope-Giver
Hospitality-Giver
Hunter

Idealizer
Importer
Influencer
Informer
Innovator
Insider
Instructor
Interfacer
Interpreter

Interrogator
Intervener
Interviewer
Introducer
Inventor
Investor
Inventurer

Jockster
Joy-Maker
Joke-Teller
Jumper
Junior

Kibitzer
Kicker

Leader
Leaver
Learner
Lecturer
Lender
Lifer
Lighter
Listener
Loader
Lobbyer
Loyalty-Lover
Lover

Maker
Manager
Manufacturer
Massager
Master
Materializer
Mender

Mentor
Mercy-Giver
Messenger
Modeler
Molder
Money-Maker
Mother
Motivator
Mover
Music Maker

Negotiator
Neighbor
Networker
Newsmaker
Noise-Maker
Nurturer

Officer
Operator
Opportunity-
    Maker
Opportunity-Taker
Organizer
Orchestrator
Owner
Overcomer
Overseer

Pacesetter
Painter
Parenter
Partner
Participator
Pastor

Pathfinder
Patronizer
Patternmaker
Peacemaker
Performer
Phoner
Photographer
Philosopher
Picture-Maker
Planner
Player
Policer
Politicizer
Pollster
Practitioner
Predictor
Preparer
Prescriber
Presenter
Printer
Problem Solver
Processor
Proclaimer
Producer
Programmer
Promise Keeper
Promoter
Prophesier
Protector
Provocateur
Preacher
Publicizer
Publisher
Puller
Pusher

Quality Creator
Questor
Quilter
Questioner

Racer
Rainmaker
Rambler
Rationalizer
Reader
Realist
Rebuilder
Receiver
Reconciler
Releaser
Renovator
Reporter
Reproducer
Rescuer
Researcher
Resourcer
Restorer
Retailer
Revealer
Rider
Rouser
Rower
Ruler
Runner

Salvager
Saver
Scheduler
Searcher
Seeker

Selector	Synthesizer	Vendor
Seller	Systematizer	Venturer
Sender		Viewer
Server	Tailor	Visioner
Sewer	Teacher	Volunteer
Scriptwriter	Team Leader	Voyageur
Shaker	Team Member	
Shipper	Teller	Wanderer
Shopkeeper	Tester	Warder
Singer	Testifier	Warrior
Sister	Theorizer	Watcher
Skipper	Thinker	Wayfarer
Solution Finder	Timekeeper	Welder
Sower	Tinkerer	Wisdom Seeker
Speaker	Trainer	Worker
Specializer	Translator	Worshipper
Sportster	Traveler	Writer
Starter	Tutor	
Storyteller		Yearner
Supervisor	Underwriter	Youngster
Supporter	Usher	

What do you do?

Now, flowing out of who you are, what do you do? Here you start to describe the specific business you are in. For marketing your business, you have to have a specific service. For instance, you communicate nothing relevant in terms of service when you say you are "in the insurance business." Insurance is not just a single business; it is a huge industry. Today that industry is a part of an even greater industry called "financial services." There are literally hundreds of thousands of jobs, positions, and services, in thousands of different companies that fall into the financial services industry. The question for you is, "what business are you in?" What specific valuable service do you provide? For example, are you a property/casualty insurance agent, health and disability specialist, investment advisor, long-term care insurance provider, estate planning specialist, employee benefits and 401K consultant. Obviously, the list goes on and on.

If you want to market your work as an advisor, you are going to have to decide on some very specific services. At this point, you might say, "well, I do a little bit of everything!" That is the problem. In broadcasting, it is often said "if you try and reach everybody with everything, you reach nobody with nothing." That little slogan demonstrates my fundamental assumption about being a good marketer: you need to have a specific service to offer to a specific audience that will benefit from it.

Take a time-out and reflect on some of the people, businesses, radio and television stations, and magazines that are most successful in their marketplace. Generally, successful businesses have either discovered or created a product or a service niche—a specific group of people who have positive feelings about the business and what they do. Finding that niche leads to the next question: "Who do you seek to serve?"

Who do you seek to serve?

Who are the people you want to work with? Choose the kind of clients you want to have. This is where the work you did in Chapter 3 can be very helpful. You will find your greatest successes as a financial advisor come from working with people who have similar interests to you. Their wish list and your wish list will have some strong parallels. The client best suited to you will share many of your same desires, values, and aspirations. Your present practice will give you an indication of those people for which you have the greatest affinity. The challenge is to give attention and awareness to the people to which you can in turn provide the most value and who can provide the greatest personal satisfaction to you as you work for them. There are coaches and advice givers out there to help you penetrate the affluent market, or to reach the business owner, or to work with professional executive types. But this is inherently a flawed and incomplete strategy.

> *"The challenge is to give attention and awareness to the people to which you can in turn provide the most value and who can provide the greatest personal satisfaction to you as you work for them."*

First of all, there are millions of successful people who that do not fit into these sought after niches. Secondly, there are great differences in these categories of people. The owner of a computer consulting firm and a highway construction company may both own small businesses. They both may be affluent but their interests, values, and desires may be very different. So do the work of describing the people in the marketplace that you seek to serve and make an impact on. Remember, choose well and you will do well.

A final thought about some potential concerns. In helping many advisors develop their marketing programs over the years I have often found great concerns and anxiety at this step. In the words of one advisor: "But there are people I might miss!" That is true. You may miss some, and that is indeed part of the program. I am asking you to choose some people and not to choose others. Here is where courage and faith come in. You must take the risk that putting your efforts into focused work on a few will be more profitable than trying to do something for everybody. This is never easy, but I assure you that as you work at it, it will become easier. Your confidence will grow. Most importantly, your income will eventually grow and grow.

> *"You must take the risk that putting your efforts into focused work on a few will be more profitable than trying to do something for everybody."*

You can also be reassured that this never becomes an all or nothing proposition. In fact, the more focused you are, you will often attract people who are out of your market but who are attracted to you due to the confidence and the expertise you demonstrate. They just come; and at that time, you can decide whether you can help them or whether you should recommend them to other colleagues. In doing this, you increase your influence and heighten your reputation among your peers. One of the marks of greatness in any profession is the ability to recommend potential clients to others, and to then be recommended by others. But now, let's go on to the most important question in your mission and marketing statement.

What do you want your clients to feel, experience, and do because they work with you?

This is the true bottom line question that is seldom answered by most mission statements, and that is why they

are not good mission and marketing statements. I remember
going into a major financial service organization, and there
chiseled in granite and marble was their mission statement.
They were very proud of it. Unfortunately, it was all about
them and said very little about the clients and customers
they were seeking to serve. I have seen this mistake duplicated in many ways and in many forms.

As I have pointed out, it is very important to know who
you are and what you do. But the most important thing to
know is how you can powerfully bring a unique, distinct
experience to the client so that they will live better and be
able to simplify their life. Traditionally, sales education
emphasized that you use features of the product to sell the
benefits. This is good advice as far as it goes. Unfortunately,
it does not go far enough in the new choice-rich experience
economy. As we mentioned in Chapter 1, people want more
than products and service benefits. They want an experience
that is enjoyable and has layers of value added. Look around
you and notice this difference. When my wife takes her auto
in for servicing, she wants more than the car repaired (benefits). She wants to feel special and well treated (experience).
When families go to McDonald's, it is not just cheap food
they want (benefits), they also want the children to play and
enjoy themselves (experience). Look around and you will see
this phenomenon in every industry sector.

So now the challenge for you in defining your business
and developing your mission statement is to know the
answers to the following questions.

- **What do you want people to feel?** Emotions are very
  important. I often say, Feelings may not reflect reality,
  but they do reflect how you feel." Traditionally financial

service advisors have been trained to present their products and ideas in analytical, rational, financial facts and figures. That is important, but financial information must give the person comfort, encouragement, and hope for safety and security. If you want people to get engaged in the planning process you are proposing or executing, you need to give time and attention to feelings.

That leads to the next part of the question:

- **What can they experience?** Here you decide what kind of reality you are seeking to help people create. This is strongly related to their feeling, but it has some reality to surround it. When you provide products and services, combined with your wisdom, warmth, personality, and presence, what does the client experience and how do they feel? Focusing on experience is the start of helping people truly enjoy the benefits that come from the products and services you provide. But there is more.

The third question:

- **What can your client do?** Here you describe some very concrete examples of what people can have and be able to do because they work with you. They can save on taxes, pay off their mortgage early, have money for a college education, be able to give money to others, have emergency income in case of an extended illness, have significant cash for their family or business in case of a tragedy, be guaranteed a lifetime of dependable income, make money with money, and leave a substantial legacy to the people, charities, and

causes they value. The list can go on and on based on
you and the services you provide,

There you have the three questions that lead to the most
important single marketing question. It is, **What do you
want your clients to feel, experience, and do because they
work with you?** When you answer this question, you have
done for yourself what would otherwise cost you thousands
of dollars from a high-priced marketing consultant. You now
have short powerful descriptions of your value to the clients
and prospects you seek to influence and serve. You are positioned. You have looked at all the potential prospects in the
population and made a choice as to which you can best
serve. You now have a way to put your value into their situation. So now, it is not about you, it is about them.

I just spoke to a client as I write this today. After doing
this kind of work, he had a number of short descriptions of
his business. He then used the key ones to describe himself
with deep precision and real passion. He reports, "they got it,
and we moved easily into the relevant client situation
without an extensive presentation and lots of fact finding.
We dealt with the issue. We should have a $40,000 commis-
sion." As I said, a good mission statement will do wonders
for your commission statement.

You can begin to do the same thing and begin to have
greater results. It will take you some time, but you will begin
to know what to say and when to say it as you start to give
your mission message. Take time to do your work so you can
be a missionary and a marketer. Like every good "missionary"
you have to believe in something and that is next.

Chapter 5
Do You **BELIEVE?**

"Be not afraid of life. Believe that life is worth living, and your belief will help create the fact." – William James

"Know what you are doing, love what you are doing, believe in what you are doing." – Will Rogers

Do you remember the old pop song by the Monkees that said, "Now I'm a believer"? If you want to be a mission-based marketer, you will have to become a believer too. Let me explain by telling you a story told to me and a few friends. An experienced and well-traveled salesman was staying in a large Southern city over the weekend in preparation for a Monday business meeting and presentation. He awoke on a Sunday morning and discovered that it was a beautiful sunny day, perfect for a long morning walk. He decided to do just that. While on his walk, he rounded a corner and came alongside what he could see and hear was a very enthusiastic evangelical church. Standing on the top of the stairs was a group of well-dressed and very happy young men and women. One of them immediately left his perch at the top of the stairs when he spotted the salesman making his way along the sidewalk. He came down to the salesman, and with intensity in his voice and fire in his eyes, he said, "Brother, do you believe?" The salesman was quite taken back by this and simply stood there, somewhat dumbfounded, and not knowing what to say. The questioner asked again with even greater enthusiasm, "Brother, do you believe?" The salesman says he then finally caught his wits, stood up straight, looked right back at the young man and said, "Yes, I believe!" He didn't know exactly what the man was talking about, but he was smart enough to know that that was probably the answer the man wanted. He was right. The questioner smiled, gave him a hearty handshake, and went back to the top of the stairs. After affirming his "belief," the salesman continued his walk.

In relating this story to me, the salesmen pointed out that even though he was not of that particular religious faith, and certainly did not appreciate their style, he was impressed by their intensity. Then after a long pause, he said, "You know what? I may not appreciate what they did; but you know, they got the question right. 'Do you believe?' "

Increasingly, I am discovering that the salesman is right. "Do you believe?" and along with that, "What do you believe?" are important questions for successfully marketing you and your professional services. Let me explain why. One of the enduring principles in personal performance marketing is attraction— "If you become, people will come." Not only will they come, but they will increasingly be the people who are a good match for you. Finding clients is called "prospecting." But attracting is more effective and a lot more fun. The question is, "Who do you want to attract?"

> *"If you become, people will come."*

To help us with this, world famous investor Warren Buffet has some insights. In his many writings and conversations Buffet repeats a central theme. Let me paraphrase it in this way: "Do business with people you like and appreciate."[1]

Buffet often invests not only in companies whose perform-ance he appreciates but also in those companies whose management, mission, and methods he also appreciates. I remember the interview Buffet had with newscaster Ted Koppel. Instead of a fancy studio, they met at a Dairy Queen in Buffet's hometown of Omaha, Nebraska. Buffet is a major owner of Dairy Queen. Why? Because he likes Dairy Queen and he respects those who lead and manage the organiza-tion. Now take this thinking and apply it to your life and business. Don't you want to work with people you like, admire, and respect? Don't you want to work with people who like, admire, and respect you? This is not some impos-sible vision. It is difficult, but it can become more of your reality if it is your intention. One of the best ways to begin to attract clients is to seek those who share similar values. In other words, do you believe the same things about life, money, and success? Because of this truth you should have a statement of your core beliefs to share with prospects and clients. Let's discuss why you should do that.

Your belief statement helps you in your marketing efforts

A belief statement not only helps you identify the people and marketplace you seek to work with, but can also provide you with a powerful marketing and promotional description and position. A belief statement helps define you and helps others better understand you. This will work well as you seek alliances and affiliations with centers of influence such as bankers, attorneys, accountants, religious leaders, and others that are in positions and places to recommend you. In some cases, it may even help you build relationships with colleagues with similar values, and who can share their success with you.

One of my clients, who was just establishing her own practice after several years with a large firm, put together a belief statement and in her networking conversations showed this simple document to others. One long time, very successful advisor, who already had a full practice and was still receiving client recommendations which she passed on to others, looked at the statement. She remarked how impressive and clear it was, and then went on to say that she would start suggesting the new advisor. My client not only had a new center of influence, but her confidence soared as a highly respected performer in the industry affirmed her. But that is only one way to use a statement of belief.

The primary way that you use this belief statement is to share it with clients and potential clients. When you are in any interview or marketing conversation, you should share your statement. Your conversation should go something like this: after you make a brief statement of your mission (see last chapter) say, "one of the purposes of our time here is that I would like to audition to be one of your advisors (or guide, coach, counselor, etc.) to assist you in making good choices about your life and your money (or investments, assets, financial goals, etc.). One of the best ways for you to discover if I might be the best one to help you is to briefly tell you some of the beliefs and principles that guide me and the way I work."

Then in a simple way, with short sentences, go through your statements. You may give a short explanation or further description of each one, or let it simply explain itself. If they make any comments or ask questions, respond as they lead or direct. If you are aware, you will get a sense of how they are connecting with you. Even more importantly, they may give you an idea of what they believe and why. That is vital to how you will eventually fit with and work with these people. Remember that we have greater trust with people who have similar beliefs to us. In effect, this may be all your presentation

". . . we have greater trust with people who have similar beliefs to us."

consists of. By the time this conversation is done, the sale might be over. They may be ready to make a move and take action. You can then go into their story and start to discover their hopes, dreams, goals, and possible strategies. You may find that you never close another sale but that the prospect closes it themselves. Isn't that a far better way to live and work?

This belief statement can also be included in any brochures that you publish. If you have a newsletter, it can and should be included from time to time. You can even write a series of short articles that give expanded descriptions of your beliefs. You may have stories that illustrate your beliefs and how they can work in people's lives. In all of these things, you are revealing more about yourself, and as the client or prospect responds, they are sharing more of themselves. The deeper the relationship, the greater the trust that begins to emerge and grow.

This statement and your beliefs become central to demonstrating that you are thoughtful, have some core positions and values, and that you have the courage to take a stand. You are not a will-o-wisp, subject to every breeze or new and hot idea. You are on a mission and you just don't say what needs to be said to make a sale. That is what mercenaries do. You are different. You are a believer.

How to start doing your belief statement

There are a variety of ways to start building your belief statement. I believe that a coach can be very helpful. It works best when you have a person who can help you sharpen both your thinking and your words. It is also important to remember that these are works and words in progress. So as you work them either by yourself or with a colleague or coach, they will become clearer to you.

As a way of coaching you for clarity, keep the following questions in mind. I often use them in my coaching and consulting practice, and their essence was given to me by my graduate advisor, Dr. George Shapiro.[2] So after you write a single belief statement, challenge yourself with these questions:

1. **What do you mean by that?** Here you can sharpen your statement, rephrase it, elaborate on it, or explain it further.
2. **How do you know that?** How did you come to that conclusion? What is the source or inspiration for your beliefs? What from your own experience confirms those beliefs?
3. **What difference does it make?** This is crucial because beliefs have consequences. So what are some of the actions and attitudes that result from your beliefs. How do they impact your life? What do they do to your key relationships? What does it mean about what you will do and what you won't do?

These are not meant to be questions to judge or attack your beliefs, they simply help sharpen your thoughts.

With these questions in mind, you start to make a list. You can begin by writing a series of beliefs based on these themes:

- **What is the meaning of success?** Almost every insurance and financial advisor claims that they are trying to help people be successful in reaching their goals. Well, what does success mean to you? We often say that if you don't know where you are going, you will end up some place else. So what is success? What does success mean to you personally? Is there a difference between what most people believe success to be and what you believe it to be? If you claim to be a success advisor, what exactly do you mean by success?

- **What do you believe about the purpose and meaning of life?** You may resist at this point and claim that you are not a counselor or spiritual advisor, you are simply a financial advisor. That may be true, but increasingly, I am discovering that as people make money, they need help in knowing what to do with it. The goal of life is not to have more money, but to have a life that has meaning, purpose, direction, and success. Money is merely a way of helping us pay the bills that come from living the life we choose, and perhaps to leave a legacy to others. Those advisors who are most successful in attracting and helping significant clients are often those who have taken some time to think about and communicate their thoughts on some of life's big issues. They then demonstrate their expertise in helping people not only do well with their money but well in their life. So what do you believe makes for a good life? I helped one advisor say this about their practice and their belief in terms of life success, "Success comes to people who live well, help others do well, finish well, and leave well." Think about what something similar might mean for you as you share your beliefs. So be a philosopher, a thinker, a life coach, as well as a first rate financial advisor.

- **What do you believe about money?** One well-known coach suggests that advisors ask prospects and clients what about money is important to them? I suggest the same question needs to be directed to each one of us. What does money mean to you? If I, as a client, am going to trust you with my future income, my retirement well-being and the dollars that will fund many of the things that I want in life, I would like to know what you believe about money. Write some statements as to the role, the purpose, and the meaning of money for you, and what you believe it could and should mean to others.

Now don't get me wrong. This is not a time to impose your beliefs upon others. Not everybody that you work with will believe exactly as you do. What this exercise does is help you define your beliefs clearly. In doing so, you will attract those people who have a similar outlook.

Recently I put a top-notch financial advisor through this exercise. After doing so, he sat in his chair for the longest time and then he said, "That's it, now I understand." In looking back over twenty plus years of his practice, he had just discovered in that moment of enlightenment that most of the clients who gave him great difficulties were those whom he knew did not share his significant values. They were people who did not see the world, money, life, and success in somewhat the same way that he saw it. We work best with those who have similar values to us. That is what I believe Warren Buffet is saying when he talks about dealing with those people whom we admire and respect.

Finally, in addition to the life and money themes, take some time to come up with some beliefs about the significant issues that affect your practice. Do you believe that most people are unprepared and fearful of good advice and planning? Do you believe that even the best prepared usually have some significant gaps in their plans and aspirations? Do you believe that financial success is never a do-it-yourself position and can only be achieved when a person seeks to have a professional team of advisors to help them? **Based on your experience, what do you believe about the financial planning process?**

When you know what you believe, you become passionate, compassionate, focused, effective, decisive, influential, and attractive. You become the kind of person you would love to have for a client. Remember, the kind of person you are is the kind of client you will get. As my salesman friend said, "I may not have appreciated their style, but you know what, they got the question right, 'Do you believe?' " Now that we have overcome our fear, created an image, know what we want, what we can do for the client, and what we believe … it's time to get that message out with real power and precision. That's next.

Chapter 6

You Have **One** Minute To Tell **YOUR** Story

"I am sorry I wrote you such a long letter, but I didn't have time to write a short one." – Attributed to Pascal

"Communication is really all anyone gets paid for ulti-mately...and if you cannot effectively communicate... you will pay...not get paid." – Doug Firebaugh

Some years ago singer Bob Dylan prophetically said, "The times they are a changing." Indeed there have been many changes in our world and in the way we live and do business. However, some things do not change. A reputation for strong convictions and values will always serve you well. A reputation for doing what you say you will do, will always be valued. Extraordinary service to your clients and customers will always be the most effective marketing tool. Those things have not and will not change. But new technology and shifting cultural attitudes will affect your business and the way you communicate in profound ways.

You are a financial advisor. The very term advisor implies that your role centers on giving people good advice. That's communication. If you are a modern day advisor, you are not just a product and portfolio salesperson. You are not just a financial planner. You are a person who communicates advice that will help people live better. Whatever other way you describe your work and business (coach, agent, counselor, planner, broker, etc), you should add "communicator." As an advisor, you not only need to fully understand the services you provide, but also the psychology of modern media communication. Communication methods have changed rapidly and they continue to do so. They affect you, your business, and your marketing efforts. Let me illustrate my point by telling a story. This is not a true story, nor is it original to me—but it begins to help us think creatively, which is fundamental to all high impact communication. It goes like this:

You have won...

One day you receive a call from an attorney in a distant state. He informs you that he has some sad news and some happy news for you. You are somewhat shaken to hear this, but you ask what it is. He tells you that he represents the estate of your Uncle Joe. Yes, the estate. The sad news is that your favorite Uncle Joe has passed away. You ask when this happened, and he tells you that he died several weeks ago. You are shocked. Why wasn't anybody informed at the time, you ask?

But even as you ask, you know the answer. Your Uncle Joe was your mother's youngest brother, very eccentric, and the proverbial black sheep of the family. He had never married, and seldom returned to the hometown area. The relationships in the family were very strained for some reason. No one in the family ever talked about it, but it was rumored that Uncle Joe had gone away and had done quite well.

The problem was that no one knew exactly what he did or what he was up to. It was the family mystery.

Nonetheless, you had always liked Uncle Joe. You are a bit of a free spirit yourself. You always sent him a card on his birthday and holidays, and called him whenever you happened to be in his city. He was always glad to hear from you, and you would occasionally meet at a cheap restaurant that he liked, and where he was obviously one of the regulars.

The attorney explained that he had helped Joe with some business dealings and had encouraged him to do some financial planning including setting up a will. Joe said that he would; but like most people, he never followed through. The attorney said that he considered Joe not only a client but also a friend. He was one of Joe's few friends in fact.

Several weeks ago, Uncle Joe had a fatal heart attack. No one knew if Joe had any family. So his employees arranged for a small memorial service and contacted the attorney. After the service he went through some of Joe's stuff, found a key to a safety deposit box. He went through all the legal hoops and opened the box. There he found a simple handwritten will. Which leads to the happy news. Uncle Joe has left everything to you, and it is a lot. It seemed that Joe was somewhat embarrassed that his work was in sanitation and junk removal—before it was called "environmental recycling." Uncle Joe's business had thrived; and with good investing and modest living, it had made him very wealthy. The good news is that you have won. He has left it all to you.

But before you begin to celebrate or do anything rash, the attorney explains that there is a strange catch to the whole thing. He explains that one of the things that Uncle Joe said in the will that he admired about you was your entrepreneurial spirit. You took the risk of not finding a safe job in some corporate womb. Uncle Joe wrote how much that meant to him, and that he knew that it is not good for an entrepreneurial type to come into a lot of easy money. It just might ruin him. So instead, Uncle Joe had decided to give you an opportunity rather than money. He has purchased a number of sixty-second commercials for your business on Super Bowl Sunday, on Oprah, on many top television programs. Indeed, you have won the opportunity to tell the whole country about the work that you do and the value and benefits you bring to the marketplace. You have an opportunity to reach millions of prospects. But like every good commercial, you have no more than sixty seconds to get your message across and to ask people to take action. In other words, you have one minute to tell your story. What would you do?

I tell that story as a way to help you understand the opportunity and the challenge that is before you as a professional financial services advisor. It is the sixty-second challenge. Today, the majority of people receive thousands of marketing messages. They ignore most of them entirely. Our brains have become very effective at blocking out the thousands of scattered, and in many cases irrelevant, messages that come to us. Most of these messages come from radio and television. They are ten seconds, fifteen seconds, and perhaps even thirty seconds long. But today, they are never more than sixty seconds. Today, most people have become accustomed to hearing all the marketing info they need to move on and move out in less than one minute. There is even some anecdotal evidence that our reduced attention span and limited time tolerance for messages may not be just what we are accustomed to by force of habit. Some scientists even wonder if there have been neurological changes in our brains. Perhaps people's minds are being rewired to the point where their tolerance for longer messages has been physiologically reduced. Whether that speculation is true, the reality is that we have very little time to get our message across today.

> *". . . we have very little time to get our message across today."*

More importantly, the little device that comes with our television set has had an even greater effect on our listening and attention habits. It is called the remote control, but what it really is is a message selector. We have become viewers who do not even wait for fifteen or thirty seconds of the message to make a decision. If the message does not strike our interest in the first five to seven seconds, chances are we will click the switch and choose a different message. The messenger, the commercial, and the sponsor better get to the point fast in order to keep our interests. If not, the listener is going to "click and switch." Click and switch. That motto needs to drive your awareness of how to speak and write today. People will click and switch unless they are quickly attracted and engaged to the message presented. So whatever your marketing messages will be, you must begin by understanding that you need to develop a one-minute message mindset. You must continually think short, concise, emotionally resonant messages. Your messages must be short, sharp, and sticky. By sticky I mean they must be memorable, make an impact, and something easily remembered. So remember, in a click and switch media rich world, our messages must be short, sharp, and sticky. In order to do this, let's start thinking like a media person as well as a financial advisor and learn some broadcasting skills and attitudes.

How to develop your sixty-second message

Successful marketing is a way of thinking as well as an approach to attracting, connecting, and bringing people to action. There are methods that can help you think and speak in a sixty-second way. In every situation you are in, you will be prepared to think and speak as a broadcaster/marketer /communicator. With this in mind, let's examine one of the long established formulas used by the broadcast media, for developing what is called "copy." Copy or copy-writing, is the script you will use in your media message. One of the favorite formulas of copywriters is known by the acronym "AIDA." It has been around for a long time. For our purposes, I have added another "D" to the formula and called it "AIDDA." Each letter in the acronym stands for a word that describes what should be our focus in crafting a powerful sixty-second commercial message.

Attention
Interest
Desire
Decision
Action

Here are what the words stand for:

"A" is for Attention

When I was in a training course at the BBC in London, one of the themes was this: "People are doing something else, stop them." Exactly. People, whether listening to the radio or going about their day, are not waiting to receive your message. They are doing, thinking, or working at something else. One of the biggest challenges for you as a financial advisor is the same as that of the broadcasting professional. We need to find a way to stop people and get their attention so that we can deliver our marketing message to them. And not only must you grab their attention, but the listener must immediately sense that there is something of interest coming to them. Otherwise they will go away. Take a moment right now to think through your day. From the morning radio, to the daily newspaper, to billboards, and everything in between, you are bombarded with hundreds of messages even before your workday really begins. All of them, in one way or another are saying "Notice me, listen to me, pay attention to me." So the first challenge that the marketer has to face in delivering their sixty-second message is how to be heard and seen amidst all the noise.

Think about this challenge and start thinking of good headlines, questions, quotes, and statements that can get someone's attention. Start now to be aware of those messages that succeed in catching your eye and getting you to stop what you are doing and think about the message. What do they do? What techniques do they use? What messages stop you? Self-awareness of our own responses to messages is

"Self-awareness of our own responses to messages is helpful in learning how they might affect others."

helpful in learning how they might affect others. Take time to watch and pay attention to those messages that are getting other people's attention. You need to be a good observer of the media world and how it works, so that you can learn how to get attention amidst the millions of pitches made every day—many of which are lost, ineffective, and a waste of time and money.

"I" is for Interest

Our brains are marvelous products of the creator's touch and perhaps millions of years of evolution. Our minds travel fast, and our thoughts quickly move on to other levels of aware-ness, and other concerns. If you have been successful in getting the listener's attention, within almost a nanosecond, the brain begins to ask other questions. It wants to know why it should keep listening. All of us lose interest very quickly if we do not find something of relevance that follows up once our attention has been captured. The sharp start to the message may have gotten us to prick up our ears, but now we will quickly turn our minds to that proverbial mindset and everybody's favorite radio station. That radio station is "WII-FM," or "What's In It For Me." Faster than any radio scanner can go, our mental receivers look for practical, helpful, thoughtful, emotional, relational, and even enter-taining and humorous significance.

The well-crafted sixty-second message must now very quickly move to things of interest to the listener. All of us have that mental, or even literal, click-and-switch device in our minds or in our hands. If the interest part of the message tails off, is weak, or fails to connect, the marketing message will be lost. It will join that long line of ignored, dismissed, and soon forgotten messages that disappear without a trace and make you increasingly invisible.

So once again, heighten your awareness of how you speak. When you talk to other people, what seems to strike their interest? When other people speak to you, what piques your interest? What are the things people say that make you mentally, even physically, lean forward? What are some of the words that keep you interested? Now you need to go deeper. No one takes significant action, solely because they are interested. From our own experience, we know that just because someone says, "That's interesting," they are not necessarily anywhere near the point where they will be ready to make any moves. So you need to take the next step in bringing your message closer to positive action.

"D" is for Desire

This is the heart, maybe even the soul, of your message making, and it is right in the center of the sixty-second message. Here you need to be deep in your understanding of the concerns, cares, fears, hopes and wishes of those you seek to help. You probably know that empathy is a vital part of significant and powerful communication. This is why those who have an empathic nature tend to be much more successful in their communication. It has been demonstrated time and time again that advisors who listen deeply and express genuine concern for their clients are far more successful in the financial services industry than those who just know their stuff. It is at this stage that your empathy, research, experience, and understanding of human nature can be put to good use. Here you seek to touch your listeners with such a picture of future possibility that they are not just

attentive and interested but are now engaged in some
emotional way to your message, and to you, the messenger.
Remember, you are not seeking just to educate the listener,
you are seeking to emotionally engage them. It is at this stage
in your message that your mission statement will be very
helpful. Your mission statement contains what you want your
client to feel, experience, and do because they work with you.
Here you need the words, the mental pictures, and the questions that ask, "Wouldn't you like to _____,"
"Wouldn't it be great to _____," "Think how better
life would be if _____."

   Here is where the listener finally connects to the message
and the messenger. The connection causes the listener to
mentally, emotionally, and perhaps in reality say, "I would like
to hear more," or "that could be nice," or "I would like to know
more," or "I want that!" It is important to know that all of these
sensations, perceptions, wishes, and decisions are happening
faster than you can imagine and often at levels of conscious-
ness that you and your listener are not fully aware of. But
when it all comes together, desire leads to the next stage.

"D" is for Decision

In the traditional AIDA model, this stage, "Decision", is
usually not mentioned. I added it because it helps you
remember that there are some powerful and productive steps
you need to be aware of. Strong desire needs to be focused
on a decision. A decision is an emotional and intentional
step to change. It is saying, "Things need to be different." A
decision means that the status quo is not sufficient, because
it is less than what you've desired. Strong decisions are
precursors to action. Most people are familiar with the world

famous Nike slogan, "Just do it." That is a call to a decision, and hopefully the action will follow. Often I coach people who have come to the point of desiring change in their life. But like most of us they hesitate, they procrastinate, and they decide to just think about it. I then say, "Write the check." That is a metaphor for making a decision in the same way that writing a check is a decision. You haven't paid the money yet, but you have decided. A decision leads to the final stage, which is taking action.

"A" is for Action

There is an old joke that plays this mind game. Three ducks are on a log and two decide to jump off. How many are left? Don't be perplexed as most are by the simplicity of the question. It is a trick. The answer is, three are left. Why? Because the ducks only decided. Decision needs to flow into action. Here we encourage the decision making by showing how you can take action.

> *"Decision needs to flow into action."*

You see, Nike doesn't teach us how or what in saying, "Just do it." They just give us the first step, which is the decision. A good marketing message must show how to execute the actions that have been decided upon based on the desire that has been cultivated, which was arrived at through relevant interest, that first of all got our attention.

Once again, you need to be a good listener to the media messages that you hear and be aware of the marketing environment. Start to listen to good AIDDA messages. You will often times hear directions on how to follow through on the decisions. For instance, you will hear "Dial 1-800 _____" or "Go to your local _____." and it will give the retail

establishment. "It is available at _____." "Take charge
_____." "Buy it now _____." "Write for _____." "Stop in
_____." These are calls to action. In many ways, these
closing stages are just that. They are the media equivalent of
the sales close. This is where we encourage people to do the
things that change their situations, even their lives. There are
many ways to do that, and our sixty-second message must
give people good directions and instructions on how to carry
out their desired and decided intentions.

Can this sixty-second message really work?

Right now you may be reading this and thinking, "No way!
You can't do that in one minute." I remember having that
same feeling when I received my broadcast training. But
then the instructors required us to do what every top
performer has to do. You practice and you keep doing it until
you get better and better. This sixty-second message idea is
not only possible, but it is done all the time, and you can do
it too. I have worked with many financial advisors who have
had just an idea in mind of their mission and the people
they wanted to serve. With this simple understanding, they
have been able to formulate a variety of one-minute
messages that are concise, clear, and comfortable for them
to say. Then as they have a clearer definition of their mission
and of their audience, they are able to modify their messages
to the situation and to the occasion in which they find themselves. As one said to me, "I really feel that I could do my
Super Bowl ad and that I could do it well." That is the kind of
confidence that comes to people who do the work of the
sixty-second message.

When you have done this work, you have a description of what you do, and you can perform your sixty-second message on the phone or in person or in any situation where it is appropriate and attractive. In addition, you can also create one-minute messages for specific services, such as financial planning, long-term care insurance, estate and retirement planning, education funding, or traditional life insurance. But there is more to it than just the message. There is great personal power in being so focused on your mission, and so clear in your message that you know you can present it in any situation. You know that you can speak in such a way that immediately gets to the heart of the matter, and to the mind and heart of the listener. When you become a sixty-second messenger, your confidence grows and your marketing efforts become easy, fun, and very comfortable. You are on the way to becoming unstoppable.

> *"You are on the way to becoming unstoppable."*

What you can do with your one-minute message

When you have created your sixty-second messages, you will have personal power and poise that will make your marketing efforts effective and fun. Here are some practical applications, and some ways to put your commercial to work for you and your business.

You can always leave a message

Unfortunately, today's financial advisor receives a lot of bad marketing and sales advice. The approach to the voicemail message is one example. Many of my clients report that they are lucky if they make live contact with one out of five completed calls. I often ask them what they do when they hear "please leave a message." Many have been taught to simply hang up and not leave one. I am chagrined when I hear that. Think about what is happening. First of all, many people have caller-ID, and when you hang up, you have already been identified. You are identified as a person who does not have the courtesy to leave a message. As a result, it will probably not go well if and when you do make a "live" contact. Others report that they leave a short message identifying themselves, their company, perhaps the name of the person who has given the recommendation, and they ask the listener to please call them back. But they leave no compelling reason for the listener to do so. They simply hope that the listener will call back out of common courtesy.

In today's busy world, few people will return a sales call that offers no reason for them to do so. Do you? If you don't, why would you expect others to? There is a better way. Use what you have learned from your commercial. When you hear "leave a message"—just do it! It is an opportunity to do, on a very personal scale, what you might have done for the Super Bowl ad. This is an ideal time to demonstrate your energy and enthusiasm. Tell them how you can make their life better, simpler, safer, and more enjoyable. In those few seconds demonstrate your focus, your wisdom, and your way with words. The challenge is to make it so interesting, fun, creative, or compelling that they call you back. Every call is now a great contact. In fact many clients now report that they

> *"In today's busy world, few people will return a sales call that offers no reason for them to do so."*

look forward to calling and that leaving a voicemail message is just fine. They do their commercial and they do it well.

You are always prepared to tell people what you do

Every day we encounter opportunities to tell our story. You will often be asked, "What do you do?" Now, this is not the time to do a full sixty seconds. But it is a time to answer that question in a short, sharp, and striking way. At a social situation, business connection, place of worship, community meeting, or even at your children's school functions, the question will come to you, "what do you do and what business are you in?" Using your sixty-second message as the foundation for your thoughts, tell them with a smile what you do. If you do it well, it may even provoke another question, such as, "What do you mean by that?" or, "How do you do that?" Now your commercial has lead to a question, which can lead to a conversation. Conversations lead to further questions. Conversations lead to ongoing connections. Conversations lead to caring for others. Conversations lead to relationships of value and those lead to sales and recommendations. Isn't that where you really want to be? It all came about because you were able to crispy, clearly, and in a compelling way, with deep conviction, tell people what you do and how you can help them.

You can have fun with creative voicemail messages

Now that you have some creative ways to respond to people when they say, "Leave a message" and "What do you do?"

You can also work with your own voicemail messaging system. Instead of recording an announcement with the typical "I'm not here" statement, say something that is clever and connects to what you do. Use it as an opportunity to remind people of your services or something else you do that the listener may not know about.

Here is a good example: "Hello, you've reached Premier Financial Services, this is Ralph. I help smart people invest for the future and save on taxes. How can I help you?" This is just one example, and there are hundreds of variations. You can design one that reflects your practice and the way you serve your clients and prospects. This is also an opportunity for you to suggest other services: "This is Comprehensive Auto Insurance Services. We make sure you never pay more than you have to for car insurance; and by the way, ask us about our auto-financing program. You can be money ahead! How can we help you?" Once again, these are just examples of how learning a variety of one-minute messages can make even your voicemail a way to market you and demonstrate just how different you are.

You make the difference with your marketing mindset

We now come back to the profound truth. What you think about, you do indeed become. What you think about a great deal eventually comes to you. These one-minute media-based messages are fundamental to getting a new mindset about what you do as an advisor. Your message of service is with you all the time. You can go "on

> *"What you think about a great deal eventually comes to you."*

the air," so to speak, at a moment's notice. One of the
reasons I ask clients to develop a number of voicemail
messages based on their sixty-second commercial is not just
so they have a variety to work with, it is so they begin to
think differently. It is so they develop a "marketing mind and
the mouth to match." I suggest you change your voicemail
message every day. Such a discipline forces you to get up
early every morning and go to your phone and think about
your clients and prospects. It causes you to truly have a
message for the day.

Doing a one-minute commercial may also give you an
idea for a marketing slogan or theme to your business. Many
advisors who have done the work of the mission statement
and the one-minute message discover a slogan that they can
use to help their clients remember them. This "slogo"
(combination of slogan and logo) is often then put on their
business cards, stationery, and all of their marketing materials. It becomes a way of distinguishing them and their
practice from all of the others out there.

Now it begins to happen. You
start becoming a mission-based
marketer. You begin to sense the
difference in your ability to clearly,
concisely, and with conviction tell
people who you are and what you
can do. You know what you believe

> *"Now it begins to happen . . . You know what you believe and how to speak it well."*

and how to speak it well. You realize that you don't need a
long brochure-laden presentation to make an impact. I have
clients whose entire presentation is their one-minute
message and a small piece of paper with their beliefs on it.
That is it. They then tell stories about their services (more
about that in Chapter 7), and ask if the prospect is interested

in continuing the conversation. If so, they continue. If not, they know with confidence that there are others who do care, and who do value them, that will come. They let the person who is not a good prospect click-and-switch and go on his or her way. They have fun, no matter what. The clients are amazed at their confidence, creativity, and attractiveness. One said, "This is amazing, they don't object any more, they just follow; and the ones who don't, I know almost immediately that they are not ready, suitable, or profitable." Those are the words of a master marketer.

As we said before, Brian Tracy said that success comes from thoughtfulness and goal setting. The rest is merely detail. We can pick up on that idea and say that when it comes to marketing, you need a mission, beliefs, and a one-minute message. The rest is detail, and that "story" is where we go next.

Chapter 7

The **Future** **BELONGS** To The **Storyteller**

"The master teacher, Jesus, came and told stories and asked questions—so what do we do? We preach sermons and give answers!" – Rebecca Pippert

"Let me tell you a story . . ." – Elie Wiesel

One of my best clients has his own paraphrase of a well-known quote about doing the same thing and expecting different results. He says, "If you do what you've always done, you will get what you've always got." To demonstrate that truth, let me tell you a story about Sam (not his real name).

Sam is a veteran financial advisor with a premier insurance and financial services company. For years, Sam was doing the presentation he had learned in agent training. He would talk about the company and its ratings, the various products and services that he could provide, and he would seek to get the client involved in a lengthy fact finder. He would then try to understand the prospect's situation and project illustrations that would solve a problem or insure an

opportunity. It was fairly traditional work, the kind that
agents and advisors go through every day. But every day Sam
was getting more and more frustrated with the results he was
getting, and most importantly, with his lack of enjoyment in
his work. So Sam and I started to work together. We decided
to do something different and see if we could get different
results.

The first thing that Sam did was work very hard on his
mission statement. He sought to determine the professional
market that he was serving most effectively and the one in
which he wished to do more. I continually asked him to
make sure that his mission centered on the things that he
really enjoyed doing and the kind of people that he enjoyed
working with. As a result of this work, Sam was able to
declare his mission and his market. He was also able to
describe the things that he was hoping that his clients would
be able to feel, experience, and do because they would work
with him. But I also continually asked Sam to "tell me more."
I asked him to give me examples. I asked him to tell me how
he had helped people to achieve the things that he had
described. In the course of our conversations, Sam told story
after story, illustrated with many funny, serious, and significant incidents where he had enjoyed helping people achieve
success, solve problems, and reach important goals. I
noticed that when Sam would do this, he was more relaxed
and was having a lot more fun.

Then I challenged Sam to really start doing things differently. I asked Sam to become a storyteller. On his next
appointment with a prospect, I asked him to take no
brochures, laptop, or illustrations. After giving his one-
minute presentation, I suggested he simply tell true life
stories of how he had helped people find solutions to the

financial, personal, and business situations they were facing. With some reluctance, Sam agreed. He had just received a recommendation to an ideal client prospect, and thought it might be best to play it safe and stick to what he knew. Nonetheless, with my encouragement, he relented.

The day after his meeting with the prospect, Sam called me. He excitedly described the amazing results of his story-telling. The prospect had agreed to immediate action within the first 15 minutes of the interview. Three days later, Sam received a thank you note from the client prospect telling him that Sam had given one of the most professional presen-tations he had ever heard from an insurance agent. The prospect became a client, opening a significant number of cases and making numerous recommendations. Last year, Sam had his best year ever in the business. He reports that he is having more fun in his work than he has ever had before. He is working fewer hours and achieving better results. Sam continually says to me in our conversations, "It's going just great." He discovered the truth that the future belongs to the storyteller. Let me explain this notion further by talking about one of the oldest forms of stories, called parables.

The power of the parable

Nick Murray is a well-known thinker and writer in the field of financial investment advising. He insists that the only real differentiation possible to any advisor is "wisdom."[1] He claims that the wisdom that you have, demonstrate, and apply in the interest of your client is the most powerful and profound difference, and the only real advantage that you can bring to the marketplace. I agree. The most significant marketing advantage you can have is your personal and professional wisdom.

Throughout history, wisdom has been communicated through stories and parables. Whether one looks at Aesop's fables or the sacred writings of the major religions, you will discover that the "wisdom of the ages" often comes to us in story form. Before great systems of theology and religion were created, the great truths of life and faith were taught and passed on through parables.

Some have said that parable is similar to the word "parabola." A parabola is a curve; and a common dish antenna is a parabolic antenna. The incoming message bounces off the curve of the disk and goes to the antenna's center receiving point. So a parable is very much like a parabolic antenna. We receive the message by an indirect means. A parable is essentially a bent message. We often get the point after it has come to us in another way. The word parable is also similar to the word "parallel," which means that the message might come alongside the listener to help them get the point. A parable is generally a story that has a point or an illustration of some significant truth or lesson. The point comes to us, often indirectly, and helps us to see what we need to see, and perhaps hear what we need to hear. If you want to be an advisor who has real wisdom to share, find ways to share stories and parables.

> *"A parable is generally a story that has a point or an illustration of some significant truth or lesson."*

For many, this idea of simple storytelling goes against everything they have been taught in profound analysis, illustrations, and financial education. So before you buy into storytelling, it might be helpful to learn some of the modern theories of communication that will help us better understand how the traditional practice of storytelling is still a powerful medium today.

Some theories on storytelling

If you are a busy financial advisor, you are probably more concerned with practical applications and results rather than any theories. But to truly explore what it might be like to be a good storyteller, it is helpful to understand what might be happening to the listener when they are hearing stories. Remember, understanding your audience and how they are moved and motivated is always going to be central to your marketing efforts. So, here are some thoughts and some theories on the art of storytelling.

Lean to the right

There is a great deal of academic research and information on the subject of brain theory. It is not only a field; it has become a virtual industry. Most of us have heard some story, information, or anecdote about right brain/left brain theory. For our purposes, let's simplify it. Later, if you want further information, you can go to the book, *Storyselling For Financial Advisors* by Scott West and Mitch Anthony,[2] or to Ned Herrmann's *The Whole Brain Business Book*.[3] It has been demonstrated that the left side of our brain is the informational, organizational, logical, articulation part of our brain. On the right side, we have understanding, imagining, risking, and feeling. The well-balanced person has a well-balanced brain. They live using their whole brain, balancing their intellect with empathy and emotions. They organize and plan, but they also understand the place of intuition and taking risks. They know how to be tough and watch the bottom line when that is appropriate, but they balance it with compassion, strong feelings, and faith. Put another way, the left leads us down the analytical road and the right leads us down the emotional path. One is clear and one is not so clear. You need to understand how to live and work going down both the road and the path.

However, every person has by temperament or training a tendency to one side of the brain or the other. Also, in certain situations, one side may emerge dominant. A simple look at your own life and how you respond to things will tell you the truth of this observation, and it will tell you something about yourself. Sometimes we use the left side of our brain, and in other situations, we are more prone to the right. But as West and Anthony point out, almost everything that the financial service industry publishes, and the advisor uses, amounts to half brain marketing and selling. Through our projections, illustrations, laptop calculations, we almost exclusively use left brain material.

So when we do things the way we usually have done them, we are not using our full brain, nor are we allowing the client and prospect to be fully mindful of what we are seeking to do. They are only using half of their brain too! We want people to take action rather not just consume information. In the financial services industry we often go down the wrong side of the mental track. We continually use left brain materials, when we need to appeal to right brain motivation. The research evidence is mounting that people take positive action because they get it, finally see the big picture, feel the benefits—the light goes on. If you have ever heard a person say, "I'll think about it," you have connected to the logical, information-based side of a person's psyche. While education is important, when it comes to taking action, we need to remember the importance of whole brain marketing and learn to "lean to the right." Stories and storytelling are an indispensable part of that marketing and communication strategy.

You connect at a deeper level with storytelling

If you take any sales and marketing training in professional sales today, you hear the same on-going theme. It is all about relationships. You are continually reminded and encouraged to remember that it is a relationship business. Yet, instead of building relationships we go back to making it an information business. If you want to build relationships, you need to do the things that will not only build but also deepen relationships. Stories can help us achieve that. Professor Mark Turner, in **The Literary Mind,**[4] suggests that human language developed out of our deep need to express ourselves and what is happening. Turner says that parables "are rooted deep in our human psyche." We connect with people at far deeper levels if we use narratives and stories to express ourselves. This is important to remember when you seek recommendations from others. The advisors who get great recommendations are often very good storytellers. They say things and perform in such a way that people truly remember them; and, in remembering them, they recommend them.

"We connect with people at far deeper levels if we use narratives and stories to express ourselves."

Storytelling helps us to think ahead

The best financial advisors continually find ways to help their client think ahead so they can seize the future opportunity and lessen the impact of future dangers. Storytelling leads us to consider a positive destiny. People make strong decisions when they have a deep sense of destiny and stories are often the way for the listener to spring ahead in their thinking. They need to imagine, see, and feel what the story will be like for their retirement, their legacy, and their family well being. Stories help us to spring ahead in our thinking so that we can take action to bring our present thinking into a future reality.

There are a growing number of books, tapes and studies, which give a greater theoretical base to my belief in the power of storytelling and why you should learn this art of the past, present, and future. Let's now move beyond theory into how to be a storyteller and how storytelling can help you make more money. Storytelling, like any art, is a matter of awareness, practice, persistence, and to some extent passion and purpose. You have to start with gaining a greater awareness of what constitutes a simple but effective story.

So if you're ready to tell some stories, here are some simple guidelines and starting points to telling good stories.

What's the point?

This is the very first thing you have to decide when you're telling a story. Your stories have to have a purpose. Every story has to have a mission. Too many times, storytelling is simply a rambling narrative of an experience. While there is a certain value in free flowing expression, when you are attempting to develop a story, you need to be very clear about the point. You don't tell people what the point of the story is, that takes away the impact. But you need to fully understand what it is you want to happen as a result of telling the story. That's the point. Once again, go back and ask those powerful mission based questions:

- What do we want people to feel?
- What do we want people to experience?
- What do we want people to do?

In short, make sure you know the purpose of your story so that your listener will get the point.

What's the predicament?

The best stories are not just narratives of events, but they're reflections and descriptions of a problem. You may remember the classic comedies of Laurel and Hardy. Oliver Hardy used to say to Stan Laurel, "Well, here's another fine mess you've gotten me into." Keep that in mind. The best stories have something that needs to be overcome or accomplished, or a situation that needs to be changed, remedied, or escaped from. So as you look towards the stories that you tell, ask yourself the question, "What's the predicament?"

People and pets make for the best stories

How would you talk about the Challenger disaster of years past? You could, as the engineers did, give details about the technical and engineering situations that lead to the disaster. You could highlight how the decision making process went awry. The story, however, connects with us when we go to the human element. The story becomes richer when we discover the lives of the people involved. Many of us were deeply moved by that incident. Not only because of the terrible tragedy, but because we also knew the stories of the people, such as teacher Christa McAuliffe, who died as a result of the accident. The tragic events of the terrorist attack on New York City in September 2001 continue to touch people as we hear stories of the people involved and how others were effected. A story is not just a narrative of events, but a description of how these events affected people. People who were moved, hurt, helped, and changed are what stories are all about.

On a lighter side, every experienced storyteller can tell you about the power of animal stories. It seems that animal stories connect with all of us. So whenever you can, think about how your story might include an animal or the proverbial family pet. This may sound very simple, and perhaps almost insulting to your intelligence, but I remind you that all of us have had deep emotional encounters with animals, either in a positive or negative way. Isn't it interesting to note that in the story of Adam and Eve, we not only had the story of God, the man and the woman, but also the serpent? Could there be a lesson in this first story?

I know one advisor who played upon his youthful appearance by beginning a number of his interviews by saying, "Would you like to see a picture of my dog?" It was very interesting to see the different reactions; smiles, laughs, bewilderment, and in most cases real interest. They did want to see a picture of his dog. Almost everyone has a dog story. The dog story lead to other stories. Then as a very clever storyteller, he was always able to find a way to have the animal story lead to people stories, and people stories lead to predicaments that called for his wisdom and his experience.

Pathos is powerful

Pathos means deep emotion. The word "pathos" comes from the same root word from which we get the word "pathetic." Often pathetic is used to describe our feelings about something and somebody that is incompetent or inept. We say they are pathetic, and what we are saying is that they are so incompetent that we feel sorry for them rather than feel any fear or disgust at their bumbling behavior. The word "pathos" does not imply such immense incompetence, but it does mean deep feeling and sympathy. In every good story, the writer, the author, or the storyteller has an awareness of the pathos in the predicament. So the good storyteller seeks to find a way to give us a person or a pet to identify with, predicament to be overcome, and deep feelings for the situation that can lead us forward.

What's the puzzle?

A good story should have a puzzle. All of us have been entranced at one time or another by a good mystery. We have all had the experience of reading a 400-page novel or watching a long movie because we want to find out what happened, "who done it," what's up, or what's going on here? This is true of every good story; it should have a puzzle. This means that when you hear a story in which you know or can easily guess the ending, your emotions will disengage and there is minimal impact. Every good story has a sense of mystery and suspense.

These are the parts of a good story. Start listening to and reading more of them. In particular, read children's stories. These well-written stories will help you to see many of these same elements that go into a good story. You will begin to discover that most people get far more engaged to a story than they do to any other source of information. Many of us have had the experience of going to our place of worship and forgetting the sermon or the pastor's message and remembering the children's sermon, which in truth was merely a good story.

How do you start?

Just do it! Do like Sam did and go back into your life, your business, and your experiences and start defining the stories behind the cases you have completed and the clients you have. If you really think about it, every significant case that has come your way has a story behind it. Or it is part of a continuing story that you and the client are creating together. I often encourage my clients to not use the word "case," but to say "story" in describing how they are putting together a particular plan, portfolio, or policy delivery. I often challenge advisors by saying "stop doing projections that illustrate and start telling parables that illuminate." So start telling stories that can help your clients and prospects see the light. You can start by identifying three different stories from your repertoire of personal experiences.

First of all, choose a story that demonstrates what you are very good at. This is fundamental to your marketing skills and relies on the business mission that you have already developed. It should be a story that demonstrates that the predicament was profound, indeed, that it was puzzling and mystifying, but through your expertise and wisdom you were able to overcome it and get to the point of a happy ending.

Secondly, you need a story that illustrates how you work with people and the kind of performance you provide. Many people believe that going through the process of financial planning is difficult and something to be avoided. Most of us do not believe that it will be pleasant. In fact, it is something akin to going to the dentist or having some similar experience. Yet, most people would like an experience that is satisfying, gratifying, and enjoyable, in fact, even memorable. Choose a story that demonstrates how aware you are of making sure that the financial advising and planning practice is pleasant as well as a powerful solution to their predicament.

Third, tell a story that helps the listener understand what people are able to feel, experience, and do, because they work with you. This is truly your bottom line story. This is your mission story. This is where we return to my friend Sam. Sam was in a face-to-face interview with that prize potential client. He was a young professional with a growing family and many aspirations. In a very simple way, Sam told the story of a client who had been in a similar situation and was able to achieve a solution. Sam told me, "I was only eight minutes into some of the storytelling, when the prospect said, "Let's start right there." The story had deeply connected. The client had seen a parallel to his situation and decided to take action. In a later reflection, Sam said that after eight minutes the commission was already up to $8,000. To which I smiled and said, "That's a pretty good rate of return." That is the end of my story.

What will be your story? Remember, the past, present and the future belong to the storyteller. Now that you understand the power of storytelling, you can do even more creative kinds of personal performance marketing. That's next after a brief intermission.

— INTERMISSION —

This Guidebook, **YOU MAKE THE DIFFERENCE,** is meant to be like a drama, a fine play, a story. It is a story of how you will become a star performer as a great financial service advisor and a great personal performance marketer. Go for greatness. We have now completed Act One; it is time for an Intermission.

An intermission is a time-out to think about what we have learned; perhaps take some time for reflection, and then to take further action. Let's reflect on our story so far. Together we have gone through fears and how they can kill everything. We have looked at how creating an image will help us overcome invisibility and how we can begin to think about and create powerful personal performance images. We have looked at the purposes and goals that will drive our life and business forward and help us be more attractive to others. These methods and strategies are also helpful to us in being a coach to our clients so that they can live lives in which they are pursuing noble purposes and great goals. We have gone through the power of a mission statement and how that can lead us to the markets that will be enjoyable and profitable for us. We have discovered that faith and belief is central not only to a life well lived, but to being a first rate advisor who attracts people of like mindedness and similar sympathies. Our sixty-second commercial has been a way for us to perform well in the modern media environment. In learning the art of storytelling, we have connected the wisdom that we have to the wisdom of the ages so that we can create wealth in the present and future.

If you have taken some time to think, plan, and are ready to act, you are on your way to being a great marketer. Many of you could stop right now, go to work, and make more money. That is because you will be thinking differently—but there is more. I remember an adult forum that I did at my church where my wife was in attendance. It was a passionate performance, where I spoke without notes or props. I poured out my heart on life, success, and spirit in making a difference. At the end of the meeting, people gathered around for questions, comments, and to say thanks. In that informal gathering, one participant turned to my wife and commented favorably on how much we had covered in the meeting. To which my wife responded, "Yes, he's just full of it, isn't he?" The double meaning made us all laugh. But there is great truth in her words. To be a good performer and a great marketer, you have to be "full of it." You have to be becoming, growing, and thereby attracting. You have to take all of the good stuff; information, ideas, strategies, suggestions, and just fill yourself with good thoughts and good things. You have to know what you believe, what you want to say and how to become all that you want to become. Those were some of the things that we learned in Act One. And now it's on to Act Two.

We need to go to the next level, to the stage and start performing. We will now overcome some other fears and talk to others in our company, our community and our world. We will learn about public speaking, broadcasting, staging

performances, even writing. We will also learn the performance art of deserving and seeking recommendations from
others. Yes, you can be and do all these things. You can be a
performer—a performer who can make a difference in the
lives of others by showing wisdom, skills, strategies, and
doing it all with a smile. The house lights are dimming; the
spotlight is ready. Act Two is about to begin, and you're on!

Chapter 8

I'd Rather DIE Than GIVE A SPEECH

"Though I speak with the tongues of men and of angels and have not love, I am become as sounding brass or a tinkling symbol." – Saint Paul

"If all my talents and powers were to be taken from me by some inscrutable providence, and I had my choice of keeping but one, I would unhesitatingly ask to be allowed to keep the power of speaking, for through it, I would quickly recover all the rest." – Daniel Webster

"The orator aims to instruct, move, and charm."
– Quintillian

Remember, fear kills everything. It is said that public speaking is the number one fear of all the fearful things that people face. According to some, there are people who "would rather die than do a talk or give a speech." I doubt that, but I do know that having to give a speech or public presentation causes great anxiety among many people. I have even known CEOs who have been fearful of giving a public talk. As a performance coach to many successful financial advisors, public speaking and presentation coaching is one of our most requested services. Most of these people can conduct a personal interview or have a conversation with no problem, yet have performance anxiety, or stage fright when it comes to public speaking. They are not alone. Many other professionals know that they need to enhance their speaking skills and overcome their fears. The popularity of the Toastmasters Clubs, the sheer number of books, tapes, and coaching on public speaking demonstrate this. If you are a financial advisor, you will need to enhance your public presentation skills. Public speaking used to be a nice thing to consider. In the future, it will be a marketing necessity.

Why you need to be a public speaker and presentation performer today

Today the world is changing rapidly when it comes to marketing, and you will not be able to connect with prospects the way you used to. You will have to become an accomplished storyteller and public speaker because many of the traditional ways of reaching people will no longer be effective. Here are some of those changes:

The telephone will no longer be your friend

A few years ago I wrote an article entitled, **"Put Down That Phone, and You are Under Arrest."**[1] The title was an attention-getting overstatement. But it contained a significant truth. Through the technology of voice messaging, caller identification, and other such devices, people can increasingly decide whether they will receive or even listen to a phone message or answer a phone inquiry. Even on the telephone, we encounter the click-and-switch phenomenon.

There is also an emerging legal obstacle to using the phone for soliciting business. Increasingly, the amount of daytime, dinnertime, and nighttime telemarketing has lead to a disgruntled population. Laws are being passed that establish no-call lists. State governments and trade associations are establishing no call lists where people say "Don't you call me, and if you do you may suffer a legal penalty." Between the technical obstacles and the legal prohibitions, it is possible that soon you may not be able to use the telephone in many marketing situations. The law may prevent you from calling and the technology may prevent you from connecting.

I now suggest that advisors begin to act as if they will not be allowed to make any outgoing first phone calls to potential clients and prospects. That may not happen in the near future, but to be well prepared for what seems to be the coming future, we should begin to adjust our thinking and our acting now.

The post office won't help you

Many marketing books and coaching programs encourage you to formulate a direct mail and letter-writing marketing program. You will get no such encouragement here. Increasingly, these programs, letters, and marketing campaigns are ineffective. Most of the people that you want to reach to build your practice do not pay any attention to such mailings. The amount of junk mail that fills the office of the businessperson and the mailbox of the successful professional homeowner is overwhelming. Junk mail is well named, because that is its destination. Let me ask you a question: what do you do with letters from people you don't know and with mail that you didn't request? Why do you expect people to respond much differently than you do?

Yes, you will occasionally find times, places, and situations where it might work. If you do enough of anything, you will get something. The question will be is it worth the effort, is it effective, and is it efficient? Another important question is "Is it any fun?" It will be very hard for many to change, but marketing by mailing will not be effective in reaching those most likely to be good clients for your financial services.

These are the two major reasons why you need to find other ways of connecting to potential clients and prospects. Telephoning and mailing will not work. Public presentations, talks, and speaking will be increasingly the platform for connecting with people about the issues and concerns that they have.

Decide now that you are going to learn and improve your public speaking and presentation skills. You will need to practice and develop a pattern for giving a simple talk. Once you learn how to give a simple talk, you will be able to give a good speech. Once you give a good speech, you can give a powerful presentation. You not only can do it, you will be able to do it well, and you will not be afraid. The following are the five questions to ask, answer, and act upon that will help you give a great talk.

1. **Who is your audience, and what do they want?**
   Every successful communicator and public speaker seeks to tailor their talk to their audience. Whenever a talented and experienced speaker is approached to give a talk, they will always ask, "Who am I talking to?" You must ask the same question. Who is the audience? What are their concerns? What do they want from this talk? Your job is to do all you can to connect to the audience. Please keep in mind that

the best talk presented in the best way, which does not connect with the audience, will accomplish nothing. Too often, we ask the question, "What should it be about?" What we need to ask "Who is it for, and what do they want?"

2. **What do you want them to do?**
   We mentioned Stephen Covey who said one of the habits of highly effective people is "they begin with the end in mind." You must do the same thing when you give a talk or a presentation. Your speech must begin with the end in mind. As you design your talk or speech, consider the listener's expectations and your hopes and ask "What do you really want people to do after they hear your talk?" What kind of effect do you want to have on them? How do you want them to feel? What do you want them to know or understand? What do you want them to accomplish? Think about these questions, because every speech or talk should have a mission. Once you have an idea of who the audience is and what effect you want to have on them, it will be much easier to build your talk. It is also at this time that you will start to use some of the same things that you learned in your sixty-second commercial. If the talk is to bring them to action, it helps to understand the impor- tance of attention, interest, desire, decision, and action. In fact, the AIDDA formula is a great outline for giving your speech or talk.

3. **How do you make it entertaining?**

   Some of you could be upset as you read this. You
   might say, "I am an educator and a professional
   advisor; I am not an entertainer." Let me explain. I
   am not saying that you have to be a comedian, but
   you need to understand that we live in an entertainment age as well as the information age. Whenever
   you are putting together any speech or presentation,
   understand that the entertainment industry and the
   experience economy have radically changed the
   listening environment, and radically changed
   people's expectations. People who might come to
   hear you, expect you to be well informed and interesting. But they probably want to be entertained as
   well. Make sure that you have a good deal of great
   content and real substance in your presentation, but
   also seek to make it amusing as well as moving. This
   does not mean you have to act silly or be hilariously
   funny or do anything that is totally out of character.
   If you do that, you will not be successful; in fact you
   are headed for a speaking disaster. But you must
   find ways to help the audience enjoy the experience
   of listening to you.

4. **What expertise do you have, and how can you
   demonstrate it?**

   When you are asked or given the opportunity to
   present a talk, you are there because you have some
   expertise in an area of interest to the audience. You
   want to demonstrate that you and the enterprise
   that you represent have a certain amount of understanding, information, and wisdom that can be

found no place else. This is not a time to brag about what you have done and can do. This is a time to demonstrate your value and the value of what you know. So as you answer these questions about the audience, your intention, and your entertainment style, also ask, "What expertise do you have and how can you demonstrate it within the subject that you are speaking about?"

5. **What are you really passionate about?**
    This is the most important. The world is full of people who have much to say and who are excited about nothing. Don't be one of those kinds of people. When you give a talk to any audience, find something to talk about in your presentation that strikes you at the very core of your being. Today, with the world situation on edge, people want to hear from a person who cares deeply about something. So when you develop your talk, on any subject, make sure you include a theme, topic, or something that you care deeply about.

    You may have noticed that I have said nothing about the subject. There are hundreds of ways to decide on a subject. You will get better at that as you practice it and as you receive good coaching and counsel on how to do that. However, the subject will come to you if you answer these five questions for the audience you are seeking to connect to.

And in conclusion...

In public speaking it is often joked that the words "and in conclusion" are what the audience really wants to hear because it means the end is near. As we come to the end of this chapter here are a few concluding suggestions. Becoming a good public speaker comes from doing good work, the good work of practice, practice, and more practice. It is not easy but anyone can do it. Good speaking requires a coach or mentor to help you. It is crucial that you find some-body who can give you honest and constructive reviews and feedback on your efforts. It is helpful to have your talks and presentations videotaped and to seek ways to improve upon them. That is why a Toastmasters or similar club is so helpful. It allows people to practice their skills in a safe and constructive place. Such a place also helps you to not take yourself too seriously. This is important because when you speak there will be times when you will fail, and in some cases fail miserably. Every great speaker will tell you there were times where their talk fell flat, the audience was bummed out, and nothing significant happened. They took it in stride, learned from their mistakes, and sought to do better next time. The most important thing they did was overcome their fears and apprehensions and continue on.

As you continue on you may discover that you and your message are ready for the media. That's where we go next.

Chapter 9

The Tape's Rolling –
Be A PERSONAL PERFORMANCE BROADCASTER To Your Clients And Prospects

"It ain't whatcha say, it's the way howcha say it."
                                    – Louie Armstrong

"If you have knowledge, let others light their candle by it."
                                    – Margaret Fuller

"Ninety percent of the success of any product or service is its promotion and marketing."   – Mark Victor Hansen

It is almost always done by computer now, but back when I first began as a radio broadcaster, the studio producer would usually say through my headphones, "Tape's rolling." It meant the tape recorder was already on, and I could start my program. As a broadcaster, I learned that the spoken word has great power to inform, to entertain, and to move people. Not only is the spoken word powerful, but today we can take our "spoken words" and literally deliver them to any space or place on the earth. Radio and television are a worldwide phenomenon. If you think about it, it is the way that most people receive their information today. Most people learn by listening to the spoken word. That has profound implications for your work as a financial advisor and being good at "personal performance marketing."

Why learning broadcasting skills could be important to you

The story of broadcasting is a fascinating history. It may surprise you to discover that when television first came into full bloom in the 1950's, many observers said it signaled the end of radio. It was consigned to the technological dump and junk heap. But with the advent of better technology, the development of the transistor, the miniaturization of radios, and the advent of FM, radio broadcasting boomed. It continues to this very day. There were further advances. Then came the Walkman®. The technology of a cassette tape player has now given rise to the CD player, and all of these things have made it possible for the spoken word to be sent, stored, replayed, and heard everywhere.

People still read books, magazines, and newspapers, and they always will. Many will find the information they seek on the Internet. But as we pointed out in the chapter on storytelling, the messages that move people are messages that are listened to and heard. People hear those messages in one-to-one conversations and in group presentations. But increasingly, people hear the message that moves them on the radio, or on a cassette or CD as they go about their day. That is crucial. Today, most people hear messages while they are doing something else: driving, walking, jogging, cooking, doing the laundry, cleaning the house.

Yet most financial advisors have no idea how to use these powerful spoken word marketing methods. They still use lots of paper, brochures, and written materials. A savvy marketer needs to know the broadcast arts and how to use the technology and methods of the electronic broadcast media. To better understand why that is true, let's take a short course in broadcasting and media theory in order to make us better marketers.

Knowing what radio and broadcasting can do will make you a better marketer

You can better market yourself with spoken words if you have some idea of how radio and broadcasting works. Radio used to be called "wireless" and that was part of the magic in it. The telegraph and the telephone were major improvements in communication. But there was that wire that had to be used. But when that wire was removed, the messages and spoken words could go everywhere and to almost any place. They could go to ships at sea and places where wire could never go. That was the power in it. That is also the power of the cassette and CD player. The spoken word can go everywhere where there is a simple receiver or a player. So for our purposes, we can speak of broadcasting in the real sense of radio, or we can speak of being a "personal broadcaster" when you reach people one-on-one with a cassette or CD. Either way, you are using the broadcast media to heighten your influence as you spread your message. Here are some of the reasons behind the power of broadcasting.

It extends your influence

When you give a personal presentation in front of an audience, or even a single person, you are using your natural senses and natural abilities. Your voice travels only as far as you can project, and the listener only hears what is in range. The great media philosopher, Marshall McLuhan, had a lot of ideas.[1] Some are very creative and others are rather convoluted. But he has helped us to understand that the media extends our senses and our capacities. When a listener hears me 500 miles away, either on the radio or as they listen to my cassette, my voice has been extended and their listening ability has been also extended. We have become so used to this that we forget how truly phenomenal it is in the history of the world. It is phenomenal, but for such a phenomenon, we pay a price. That price is that by extending one human capacity, our ability to speak and be heard over long distances, we lose others. We are not able to see or feel each other. Nonetheless, when you produce a program for a radio, an audio cassette or CD, your power to reach out and connect has been extended perhaps hundreds or thousands of times beyond your capacity to shout or your listener's ability to hear. It would take a great deal of time and energy to have to repeat your message over and over for listeners who would want to hear it at different times, but now you can do so without any extra effort. Broadcasting extends you, your message, and your influence.

"Broadcasting extends you, your message, and your influence."

It heightens the experience

There is no question that the printed word can be very
powerful. The spoken word has even greater power. The
printed page with words is literally, and in many cases, expe-
rientially flat. It is the spoken word that can have emotion,
power, and life, far beyond the print. You can read the words
of Winston Churchill and Martin Luther King, Jr., and be
inspired. But when you hear them, it is to feel the very power
that can move you. Even today, after having read it many
times and heard it many times, a recording of Martin Luther
King, Jr.'s "I Have a Dream" speech still moves me. I get the
proverbial goose bumps, and sometimes, have been moved
to tears.

The spoken word also gives you the
power of the pause. You can pause to
gain attention. You can also speak with
greater emphasis and project your
feelings, be they sad or happy. So when
you go into the broadcast mode and
into the spoken word, you are extending your impact. It is
greater because of the experience that comes from speaking
and being heard.

> *"The spoken
> word also gives
> you the power
> of the pause."*

It saves time

The broadcast media allows the listener to save time. You
can listen to the news while you are doing something else.
You can drive to an appointment and learn about the latest
marketing strategies on a cassette tape. Most of us in this
business have already been told that we should turn our
drive time into learning time. You can do the same thing for

your client or prospect. You could say to a client or prospect, "Here is a program just for you about how to choose mutual funds for your 401(k) plan. While you are on the road, take ten minutes to listen and tell me what you think." This leads to a related point: the message is portable. You can not only be doing something else, you can be some place else when you share the message via broadcasting. People love to save time and when you become a broadcaster, you can help them do it.

Broadcasting gives people choices

We have already learned about the click-and-switch principle. But there are even greater choices that we have and that the listener can use. The listener can decide when and where they will listen. The cassette or CD can be popped in any time. They can choose to listen with others or they can choose to listen by themselves. They can choose to listen in private, or they can share it with others. People have a more favorable response to any message when they feel they have a greater freedom to choose. We have all been in situations where we felt captive to the speaker. We may want to leave or to take a break, but we can't. Think how uncomfortable that makes you and how unreceptive you are to the message. A personal broadcaster, however, allows the listener greater freedom and greater choices. I often point out that a salesperson may try and close down choices, and even coerce a decision from their listener, but a great marketer knows better than to do that.

It can be very personal

I still remember many of the responses to my radio
programs. In some cases, there were thousands, perhaps
millions of listeners. But when I was performing at my best,
the response from the listeners indicated that they thought
that I was talking just to them. It was not uncommon to hear
a listener say or write, "Wow, that message was just for me.
How did you know I was listening today?"

The powerful paradox of broadcasting is that as you
speak to the many, the listener often feels that they are the
only one involved in the conversation. It is not uncommon
for people to believe that they are the *one* you are talking to.
This is the greatest power of the broadcasting arts. Even
though your senses have been limited and only one has been
extended, the degree of power, intimacy, and personal
engagement between you and your listener can be overwhelming. As I mentioned in my introduction, you can
always say, "This is for you."

This is just a very brief summary of radio broadcasting
theory and how you can use it. Let's move on and discover
some of the ways you can use these ideas to be a better
performance marketer.

Receive some coaching or training

You might take this whole thing very seriously and actually
enroll in a broadcast course at a technical or community
college. Here you would learn some of the basics of
announcing and program production. You would also learn
some of the same techniques we learned in our one-minute

message. You would also be challenged to expand your vocabulary, watch your pronunciation, and better under-stand some journalistic practices so that you could report on local, national, and world events. If you have the time and money to do this, it might not only be helpful in your marketing but also give you other venues to expand your personal influence.

However, there are other ways that you could pursue less formal but just as effective training. You could do as many of my clients do—engage a coach to help you learn the basics and achieve your specific goals. The coach would help you in learning some of the basic broadcasting skills and acquiring some broadcasting attitudes. But before you do any of these things, consider some of these suggestions and exercises that will help you on your own.

Be aware, listen, and practice

Practice listening and speaking as a broadcast performer. Every great performer in any field has to practice. Performance marketing and broadcast speaking is performing. So make a commitment to practice. Take time to listen, really listen to those television and radio performers who do an excel-lent job. Don't just listen to what they say, listen to how they say it. Try and imitate them from time to time. Pay close attention to how they use their voice. Notice the tone they use in their voice, their pausing and their pause for effect, and how they make a point of not going up in pitch at the end of a sentence. In broadcasting, this is called finalization. Many of these things will not be immediately evident to you. But

"Don't just listen to what they say, listen to how they say it."

when you are fully aware, you will begin to notice some of the ways that a trained broadcaster speaks differently than the average speaker. You will also notice that just because somebody has a radio job does not mean that they are well trained or polished performers. As one of my clients said after receiving some broadcast training, "I could do just as well as that person is doing." He is now expanding his financial practice and enhancing his community reputation by doing an outdoor radio program on a local station. He was right. He was better than many on the radio, and he believed he could do just as well if not better.

Start to notice who is good, who is ordinary, and who is poor and most importantly, what the difference is. Practicing this focused awareness is the first step in being a top performer. Also take time to select a few announcers or broadcasters that can be real models for you. Try to imitate them and hear how it sounds, and notice how it feels. One of the best ways to be a good speaker is to be a great listener.

Now start to practice speaking like a good announcer. This doesn't mean that you should try and be anything or anyone but you. Be you, yet seek to be a professional sounding speaker and reader. Have fun with this. You should get a simple music stand and purchase a simple broadcast tape recorder or mini-disk recorder. Very satisfactory recorders and microphones can be purchased for $200 to $300. Then go to the Internet, newspaper, or magazines and find materials to read. If you would do fifteen to twenty minutes every other day of practicing reading and speaking as a broadcaster, your reading, speaking, and thinking will become much clearer. Then take the tape that you made and take it with you as you go about your day in your auto. Listen, and notice how you would do it differently. This will not take lots of time or money and the reward will come in you speaking with increased power and confidence.

Here are some other things to be aware of that will improve your performance

Watch your breathing

One of the marks of good performance broadcasters is the quality of their breath control. If you've had any voice training in singing or speaking, you know how important breath control is in good modulation, projection, and voice tone. It is even more important in broadcasting, because the only thing people are sensing is your voice. There is another factor. The microphone is only three to six inches away and it catches any breathiness or loud "up" breathing as you speak and catch your breath. The more you can use your abdomen to breathe and the less you use short breaths, the better you will sound. Your voice will also have a deeper pitch with better resonance. As you do this, seek to relax your chest and throat. Often when we get nervous, we breathe shorter breaths from the top of our lungs, and our throat muscles tighten up and constrict. That is like forcing our speaking breath through a flute. The smaller opening makes for a higher pitch. We may even squeak like a clarinet if we get too nervous. So be aware of your breathing and just relax.

Speak clearly

In broadcasting, we often called it "Monday mouth." After a weekend of not being "on-the-air," our mouths would get lazy. That is right; we would not fully open our mouth. In just a few days off, we would get sloppy in our articulation and enunciation. Oftentimes we had to take special attention to warm up and get back into the mode of speaking clearly, enunciating, and articulating our message. It is very likely that unless you are very aware, you are speaking with Monday mouth all the time. You are probably not speaking nearly as clearly as you could. We tend to hem and haw and say "ah." When you go to a broadcasting course, one of the instructor's most frequent comments will be to open your mouth, articulate, and watch your hissing S's and popping "P's." All of these are ways to say "Speak clearly."

Be real, be you, and have fun

One of the common sayings in broadcast training is, "You can hear a smile." Indeed, you can. A good and pleasing broadcast voice comes from a smiling face. The key to good communication is not just good information but positive energy. Remember our discussion about image? Well, here is an opportunity to revisit that idea. Your voice image should flow naturally from your personality. Those who communicate well in the media are not hyper or outrageous personalities. Those who do that are entertainers, not necessarily communicators. The best broadcasters are aware that they need to enhance their personal presence and persona via their voice. They are aware of cultivating, not creating, their distinct personality. Indeed, the best of them make sure that there is a person behind the voice.

Now roll the tapes . . .
and be a personal broadcaster to your clients and prospects

I once heard a story about a man who wrote a novel just for practice. He was an aspiring author who decided to become a writer and call it his day job. Every evening he went to work as a bartender to pay the bills and get ideas for characters and stories. The interesting part of the story was that he had no intention of publishing this novel. He knew that most first novels were not that good and the chances of being published were very small. So he wrote an entire novel just for practice. I tell this story to suggest a possible strategy. If you've been with me this far, you have learned some basic but important material about marketing communication and broadcasting. This will make you a better media consumer and a better marketer. Even if you have no intentions of trying to be on the radio or to produce an audio program, simply understanding some of these ideas will make you more effective in your personal and group presentations. It will also make you a better communicator just because you learned how to practice. I have worked with advisors who enjoyed the exercise of doing a simple audio program with no expectations other than learning about themselves, how to market themselves better, and enjoy the process. They made their programs and distributed copies to a few friends, clients, and prospects. They told them that they were just practicing and wanted their response. They had fun. With some of these cases, they discovered they had a winner, and then went on to better things and did better programs.

That may be all you really want to do, just practice and become a better communicator. But if you would like to start being a personal broadcaster using some of these principles and practices, let me conclude this chapter by giving you some simple strategies using audio cassettes and CD's in your marketing practices.

Don't talk about you, help them

I have listened to many audio-tape programs done by agents and advisors. Many of these have been well done and the results outstanding. However, most of them make a very serious mistake. The entire tape is either an interview or a program that is all about the advisor. It is nothing more than a lengthy commercial. Again, I ask the question, would you ever listen to a twenty minute commercial about somebody else? The answer is obvious. Put yourself in the place of the listener. Why would a client or prospect want to spend twenty minutes of their time hearing about you? So don't talk about you, but give valuable information that will be helpful to the listener. A short audio program should include helpful and valuable advice and information. It should tell stories that the listener can use to make their life simpler, safer, and better.

> *"Put yourself in the place of the listener."*

One advisor explained how long-term care insurance works and the things a person should consider in purchasing it. Other advisors explained what goes into financial planning and how helpful it can be when done well with a professional advisor. Another produced a highly informative program that talked about all of the various scams and schemes that attempt to swindle older retired people out of their money. It was extremely helpful to those people, and many clients and prospects expressed their appreciation for it. It literally saved some of them thousands of dollars. The tape was passed on and on and on. One advisor interviewed one of the top estate-planning attorneys in their community. It was a very informative interview, and it benefited both the advisor's practice and the attorney. It was a proverbial win—win—win.

These are just a few suggestions. There are many other possible programs that any competent financial advisor can plan and introduce with a little thought, practice, and production help.

Keep it simple because they cannot see

I often reminded my colleagues and trainees when I was in professional broadcasting that radio is a "blind medium." An audio program extends the speaking and listening ability of the speaker and hearer, but they are both blind in that they can't see each other. That means that you learn how to speak using simple statistics and facts. As a broadcaster you learn that you cannot rely on charts, graphs, illustrations, and pictures to get your points across. You have to use stories, metaphors, and word pictures that help people understand the concept rather than get deeply involved in the details. As I remind every aspiring broadcaster, "you have to help them see by hearing."

Make sure you test your program first

One of the fundamental rules of marketing is testing. After you have made your program, don't make hundreds of copies until you have tried it out first. In working with your coach or producer, produce a simple pilot program and make a few copies that you can hand out to clients, colleagues, and friends. Ask for their honest response. In some cases, the simple test marketing itself will tell you something about the program. You discover ways to improve it. You may find that the very test marketing itself will bring some results. Then you can approach the duplication process with real confidence, knowing that you have already received a good review for your program. On the other hand, if you discover that there are significant things that you can improve on, you can go back into your studio and make those corrections and additions. You then can feel greater confidence in the quality of your program.

Don't make thousands of copies of your audio program ever!

Today you can have a studio or a duplication facility produce very small quantities of tapes and CDs. Your program may have to be, and should be, updated and personalized often. I have seen it happen many times. Thousands of cassette audio programs that are now out of date, out of compliance, and on the floor of the garage, are a nightmare come true. This does not have to happen. I have a client who updates his audio program every year. The duplication studio produces them in batches of twenty, whenever she requests them. In testing the program first, we found that she did not need the fancy and expensive cover. In fact, a simple story card brochure along with her cassette in a plastic case worked just great for her prospects.

Make it very personal

One of the most powerful things about broadcasting communication is that it can be very personal. Even though your audio program is on a subject matter that is of interest to

"One of the most powerful things about broadcasting communication is that it can be very personal."

many people, it can have the feel of being very personal.
However, there are situations where you can literally make it
even more personal.

One advisor had extraordinary success by putting
together a personal audio program for a large family that
was coming together for a meeting in order to decide on the
estate plan for the family business. Think how impressed the
family was when they each received a very professional
cassette program, specifically addressed to them and to the
issues before them, that they could listen to prior to the
meeting. This was a large case, and there were many advisors
competing for the privilege of working with the client. Guess
who got the business?

Now, this program was produced in a studio and
sounded very professional. However, you can produce all
kinds of personal programs for clients and prospects without
going to a recording studio. I suggest that advisors set up a
small recording situation in their office. This is very similar
to the one that you constructed to practice to be a broadcaster. Very good quality can be had with a very modest
investment. After you have a conversation with the prospect,
go back to your office and make a personal tape to them in
which you summarize the conversation and make some
reflections on their situation. You can give some pre-
approved by compliance information and yet make it very
personal to them. You enclose a note saying that it is only
seven to ten minutes long, and they can listen to it in their
car. You can even make a personalized cassette or CD label
with their name on it. All this can be done very easily and at
minimal cost.

One advisor that I know has even made a tape where he
helps people fill in the information form necessary for him

to prepare a financial plan. Some advisors are now even preparing an audio newsletter that people can listen to. In fact, such a newsletter can often be produced for the same price and in far less time than a conventional printed newsletter. In the near future, since the technology is already available, you will also be able to have personal audio programs on your Web site or sent through e-mail. This will allow you to communicate with greater impact and even save on the cost of transportation, as well as tape and CD production. The possibilities are endless.

But most importantly, you can have fun as you make more money. These personal radio programs not only provide helpful information to clients and prospects but they also allow you to project your warmth, your wit, and perhaps provide some

> *". . . most importantly, you can have fun as you make more money."*

entertainment. One advisor who has adopted this marketing format said to me, "I've never had so much fun in my life marketing my practice, and I'm getting extraordinary results." Perhaps it is time for you to consider the power of being a personal broadcaster.

Now that you are comfortable speaking to many people and using the broadcast arts, you might want to consider the dramatic arts. That is next.

Chapter 10

It's Your Turn
In Your Town
And You're
On Stage

"At the end of each day you should play back the tapes of your performance. The result should either applaud you or prod you." – Jim Rohn

"Everything in life is theater." – Mayo Jones

It was the last act of our high school production of Thornton Wilder's **Our Town.**[1] My small part was in the last scene, and the assistant director whispered, "Okay, Stan, you're on." I knew that after weeks of rehearsal the time had come to perform. These and other opportunities to perform gave me the self-confidence that helped me in my later life as a teacher, missionary broadcaster, and now a performance coach. Many of you have had similar experiences as actors and thespians. Let's learn from the dramatic arts and remember that it's time for you to be "on in your town."

It's about the experience

In Chapter One I discussed the book *The Experience Economy: Work is Theatre, & Every Business a Stage*[2] by Joe Pine and Jim Gilmore. They claim that the dramatic model has grown in importance due to the development of a new business reality called the experience economy. Let's do a brief review of their claim that what clients and customers value has changed. Today, and in the near future, successful businesses will be those who understand that clients and customers are seeking an experience. Experiences are created and marketed when the people in the business enterprise think of themselves as performers—their work as theater, and their business as a stage. Financial advisors need to know how to perform in the experience economy. Let's describe how financial advisors can do that.

You turn talks, seminars, and presentations into performance events

It is with a dramatic model and experience economy perspective that you can begin to put all of your perform-ance marketing pieces together. When your image and style are complemented with deep beliefs, convictions, life purposes, and expertise, you become attractive in the very best sense of the word. When your marketing scripts are clear and convincing, your power grows and your fears subside. Now put storytelling, speaking, and broadcasting together in a way that allows you to take marketing to a whole new level—the level of the stage performance. Here is how that works for you.

For many years, many advisors sought to build their business through seminars. In the industry, it is often called "seminar selling." This marketing strategy is time tested for some, and to some extent it is already timeworn. This is usually how it works. You either buy an approved program on a relevant topic or design one of your own. You seek a place to present it, ways to advertise it, work to fill the seats, and then present it. You then seek to go from the seminars to making appointments to selling your products and services. Many have experienced great success with this approach. Others have found the whole process overwhelming and not very profitable.

Obviously there are mixed opinions and very different results. This should come as no surprise. Remember, if any of the so-called marketing solutions were truly solutions, your problems and my problems would be over. We would just follow the recipe and the revenues would follow. Seminar selling will continue to be effective for some. But it will be less so. The trend has passed. Many in the market-place now recognize the seminar for what it often is, simply a sales event. They either avoid it or use the information there to seek ways to do it themselves. In many cases, they literally steel themselves against the sales pitch. They know it is coming and they are ready to resist.

Let's consider ways to turn the seminar into a perform-ance and the performance into an experience. I do not have a recipe, because marketing recipes seldom work. Here are some things to consider. Have a broader vision of what you could do. A seminar is a class, an educational event. It provides the participant with information. Now what might happen if you combine the information with a program that could be interesting and even entertaining? What if you had

"Have a broader vision of what you could do."

a program with music and stories on growing up in the 1940's and 1950's? Then a testimonial from a person who bought long-term care insurance and how that saved money and a family legacy. Then you, the program sponsor, give a simple, belief-packed short talk on the things you need to consider when you buy long-term care insurance. Such a program might be a lot more fun than a 90-minute PowerPoint demonstration. Think about the possibilities. Remember, the point of a program is not to fully educate the audience but to energize and emotionally involve them so they trust, listen, and seek out your wise counsel.

". . . the point of a program is not to fully educate the audience but to energize and emotionally involve them so they trust, listen, and seek out your wise counsel."

Here's another idea, which you can perhaps customize for your own purposes. You have the opportunity to give a presentation for a 401k or a 403b program at a company or school. Instead of the usual graphs and performance illustrations, do it differently. Think of bringing in a small stepladder and an actor. Tell a story about Ms. Investor who wanted to reach the sky and decided to invest all of her resources for her retirement income by herself. So she climbed to the very top of the ladder. She stands on the step that warns, "No Step." She falls (you need a good actor and a bit of an athlete), and vows never to do that again and puts all of her money in the bank where she earns a small interest dividend. She in effect "loans" money to the bank at 4%, and they loan it to her friend down the street at 15%.

You the advisor step in and say, "something is wrong." You take the ladder and do it differently. On each step of the ladder you put signs with names of various funds. Step one is a Conservative Fund. Step two is Value and Moderate Risk. Step three is Aggressive Growth. Then you point out that there are people who call themselves investors who are really nothing more than speculators and gamblers. That is the very top step. What does the top step say? It says, "No Step." Your promise is that you will never ask nor suggest that they do that. With you they can choose the level on the ladder that matches their tolerance for risk in their investment program. This is how you illustrate risk, educate, and describe the opportunity that an employee-qualified plan has; and you do it while having some fun. You then briefly give the details and ask those who are interested to follow up, get with the program, and start climbing the ladder to success with the steps and at the pace that is comfortable for them. You end the program by providing them refreshments. Now think how you might take this idea and create a program that matches your style, your audience, and your content whenever you have a group enrollment or a presentation for any of the various services you offer.

One of my friends is a gentleman named Denny Zahrbock from Wayzata, Minnesota. He has produced a show that he has given for a number of clients and demonstrated to many of his colleagues. You have to see Denny's show to fully experience the power of it. But in his program he explains business succession and estate planning with a simple and entertaining program. Denny arranges for an appointment with someone who he has been encouraging to take action on a vital estate or business planning issue. He comes to the office equipped with a duffel bag full of cash. He makes his entrance and gives an introduction. He says that he wants to illustrate what they are doing. He then puts a whole bag full of real cash on the desk and says, "This is your estate. When you die, this is what will happen." He picks up half of the cash and throws it away. The person is shocked. Denny then suggests that they pick up the cash and put it back on the table. He then takes a small percentage of the cash that is on the table and suggests investing it in an estate plan that will make it possible for something powerful to happen. By doing this, instead of your cash going to pay the estate tax bill, the tax bill is paid by the proceeds from the insurance company.

You may not be able to do exactly what Denny does, but his idea can start you thinking as to how you can turn a personal presentation or seminar program into a stage performance. You can not only tell an engaging story but perform it in such a way that creates an impact and moves the prospect into taking action. Whenever you present a seminar or program, seek ways to use stories, props, and action demonstrations to highlight important points and to lighten up some of the heavy stuff. You can also seek ways to get the audience involved. These ideas may not be ones you'd care to copy, but use them to spur your own creativity. You can produce custom programs that help the audience to remember you.

Create a stage

Any place where you perform becomes a stage. Whether you are in a client's home, their office, or an auditorium, that is your stage. You need to constantly be aware of how you can use simple props and empty spaces as a stage. But you can have even more control of the experience and set the stage in your own office. Most advisors will agree that having prospects and clients come to the office is a better way to work with them. There you have all of the material that you might need and can meet any contingency. It can also save a lot of travel time and trouble. In many ways, it also positions you as a professional along with doctors, attorneys, and accountants. Most of them ask that the client, prospect, or customer come to their office. We should seek to do the same, and one of the best ways to do that is to think of your office and conference room as a stage where you perform. Here are some ways you might do that.

> ". . . think of your office and conference room as a stage where you perform."

First of all, consider taking down all of the sales awards that you have. You may be very proud of them, and they are well deserved. But think about what they might unintentionally communicate. They might be saying to the client or prospect, "Watch out, you are in the presence of a salesperson!" Service and community awards are always an important part of who you are, but selling awards may not be the best message to put in front of the prospect.

Now that you have removed some of the sales awards, what should you do? How about replacing those sales awards with pictures of clients who have achieved success in reaching their financial goals? One of my clients, a long-term care insurance specialist, has photographs of clients who are fully enjoying their retirement now that they have no fear of losing their retirement income to pay for possible long term health care. The pictures are fun and engaging, and there is a story behind each one. You can then use the stories behind the pictures as a part of your presentation. Collections of all kinds are always conversation starters and experience enhancers. I have had clients who have furnished their stages with everything from antiques to golf clubs to toy farm tractors. What kind of collection could you have that would begin the storytelling, enhance the experience, and be of interest to those with whom you work?

I have clients who have decided that making the experience fun was a part of setting the stage. One advisor had an old fashioned pinball machine in the office. Many of his clients loved it when they came in for their appointments. He told me of one distinguished older woman who was playing the machine and with a smile said, "When I was a girl playing one of these things was a sin and not done by a proper young woman."

Another friend who is a golf enthusiast has even put a small putting hole and flag right in the office. Perhaps some of these ideas will get you thinking about your stage. But even if you don't go to these measures, there are small details to which you can attend. Why not have good china and gourmet coffee rather than that office stuff in cheap Styrofoam cups? Give full attention to plants, flowers, and works of art and seek to make them consistent with your style, image, and even better, make them part of your story. Go even further, and plan some performance scripts and the proper stage movements for your staff and colleagues. When clients and prospects come to the office to meet you, does the receptionist stand and greet the guests? Do they know how to welcome them and thank them for coming? Remember the great line from Cheers? "Everybody knows your name, and they're really glad you came." Are you doing all you can to heighten the

"Are you doing all you can to heighten the experience by simply letting people know how important they are . . . "

experience by simply letting people know how important they are by knowing their name and expressing delight that they came?

Another client has an office in an historic building. Part of the experience of the building is that the elevators are still operated by real people. Think of what you might be able to do with that. If an important client or prospect is expected, give a heads up to the operator with a description and the time of their possible appearance. (It might also help to do a favor for the operator from time to time.) When those people come into the elevator and give the name of the floor or most likely the name of the firm, the operator can say, "Are you Mr. and Mrs. Smith?" If they acknowledge that that is who they are, the operator can say, "They have been expecting you." Do you understand the power in those simple words? I can image it is a memorable experience.

Now you might not have a personal elevator operator in your agency, firm or office. But everyone can perform in the very same way. Everyone from partners to associates to assistants can be equally well scripted, and know their stage movements in such away to make the guests feel important and welcome. One of my clients, who has carefully combined many of these elements in their practice, simply said, "yes, we are very good at what we do, and we put on a good show too."

Peter Brook, a world class director and drama critic, wrote a book on theater called *The Empty Space.*[3] His point was that any empty space could be turned into a stage where performances could take place. The challenge is to turn your space into a performance stage where people fully sense and experience that you, your firm, and your colleagues are the difference. Once again, these are some ideas that have worked for others. If they are to work for you, they must be consistent with your style, your image, and the things that you hope to create. But they are done with a simple mission of making each person feel that they are very important. Pine and Gilmore even demonstrate that an "experience" can be created by knowing how to take a very positive client service idea and customizing it for the specific client or prospect. When the service is delightful and says, "this is for you," things happen, people take action, and people change.

Finally, using style, scripts, performances, and a stage is a way to bring all of the performance elements together. Clients and prospects will see you as bringing to them a unique and compelling experience, and they in turn will bring others to you. As one client said, "I never need to ask for any referrals, because my clients just send others to me all the time." That is the power of personal performance marketing in the experience economy.

There is even more we can do to enhance the experience. Using electronic technology to connect and engage people with our expertise and wisdom is where we go next.

Chapter 11

Be A Writer
And A **Powerful**
MARKETER

"If we had to say what writing is, we would define it essentially as an act of courage." – Cynthia Ozich

"Everybody is talented, original and has something important to say." – Brenda Ueland

A deep desire . . . to be a writer

Some years ago, the Beatles sang about a "paperback writer." In some ways, that song plays to a favorite fantasy. Many of us would like to be a writer some day. We hear of J.K. Rowling going from welfare to millionaire as the author of the Harry Potter books, or of Frank McCourt, a retired schoolteacher, who became a celebrity as the author of *Angela's Ashes.* We wonder "could that be me some day?" If so, you are not alone. There is a whole industry of small presses, agents, books, and magazines targeted for "wannabe" writers and authors. For many there is a deep desire to possess thoughts and ideas worthy of print and paper and publication. A desire to write may in fact be a part of what it means to be truly human.

This wish may come from the deeper desire to be significant—to make our mark in our world. We may want to create something that is lasting and meaningful. The spoken word, as we said, is very powerful. But the written word may be more influential and long lasting. The desire to be a writer may also come from our desire to be creative and to connect with others. Maybe it is part of the "God-image" within us. All of these speculations may be amusing, and even close to some truth, but when it comes to marketing our business, we can move from transcendent speculation to some very practical applications. Writing and publishing is a significant part of personal performance marketing and in demonstrating that you are different, unique, and influential. Let's continue with that idea.

> *"Writing and publishing is a significant part of personal performance marketing and in demonstrating that you are different, unique, and influential."*

Writing and publishing are powerful marketing tools

Dr. Thomas Stanley, author of the best selling books, *The Millionaire Next Door* and *The Millionaire Mind*,[1] has done extensive work in researching the best ways to network with and market to the affluent population and affiliated groups. Many of his important principles are focused on that market segment, but they apply to many others. In a tape program entitled, **"Networking with the Affluent,"** Stanley gives us a slogan to help us remember what we should aspire to do in our marketing efforts. He says, "Talkers are hawkers, and writers are experts."

What does that mean? Stanley does not mean to denigrate those who speak and sell, but to point out an issue of perception when it comes to professional services and our reputation. We tend to believe that those who are really expert in their work and masters of their craft have been noted and quoted. They have been published. They are respected for their ideas and their influence. Even when we hear a speaker and are impressed with their words and message, their credibility is often enhanced and reinforced by noting and citing their publications—the books and articles they have written. In fact, many speakers would not make it on the speaking circuit by their speaking skills alone. It is because they have a reputation based on their publications. Whether all of these perceptions are fair is not the issue. The perceptions are market realities. Those who can write and perform as reporters, reviewers, and thinkers will find that they are far more attractive to those who want expert and reputable advisors in their life and business.

Today's E-Mail makes it easy to become that kind of an advisor

One of the best ways to start writing and being noted is to understand the possibilities in e-mail. E-mail is changing the way we communicate and therefore it is changing the world of marketing. Thanks to e-mail, you can easily connect with prospects and clients and become a writer and publisher at the same time.

Jeffrey Lant of JAL Associates from Cambridge Massachusetts, a marketing consultant with over twenty-five years of experience, boldly said that he now speaks of his business in terms of "A. E." and "B. E."—"after e-mail" and "before e-mail."[2] He claims that the e-mail phenomenon has so radically changed the marketing landscape that many long time strategies are now obsolete. Could that be true? To consider that, let's look at some of the advantages of e-mail for connecting and communicating:

- It provides almost universal access to people, at their convenience and with their permission. Because e-mail should only be used with the receiver's permission (more on "permission marketing" later), smart performance marketers never SPAM. (It ruins the experience.)

- E-mail saves on costs. There are no postage, printing, or paper fees.

- Since the receiver of any e-mail chooses whether to delete, read, or print the document, the only paper you use is what is needed. This eliminates all junk mail paper, and it is more environmentally responsible.

- It provides instantaneous communication at any time and as often as you wish.

- It provides interactive communication. The receiver can respond and state their opinions, feelings, ask further questions, and share their own explanations.

- Powerful and compelling visual graphics and video programs can be attached and included on e-mail messages. Immediate links to other pieces of information and related web-sites can be a part of an e-mail message.

We are just starting to discover all of the possibilities. For these and yet to be discovered reasons, e-mail is not the way of the future—it is the present and will change the future. Right now, you can use it to become the expert, a writer that clients and customers value.

Start writing an e-newsletter. You may eventually write books and articles, but you can start by doing a newsletter and by giving it away, and distributing it by e-mail. A newsletter is a perfect fit for your ongoing personal perform-ance marketing program. First of all, it does what Thomas Stanley says is very important; it positions you as an expert. Next, it gives you the opportunity to demonstrate your wisdom and experience. Finally, it expands your influence. It extends your thoughts and ideas. Newsletters travel great distances. In the e-mail format, they are easily forwarded to and shared with others. I have been fortunate to have several advocates who regularly forward my e-newsletter to their friends and associates. The same thing will happen to you if you demonstrate wisdom and deliver value. The newsletter is a way for your influence to grow and your visibility to increase.

Doing a newsletter just from you

When I suggest a newsletter as part of an advisor's marketing program, I get a variety of reactions. Some claim that it would be too much work, and not worth the trouble. Others say they are thinking of using one of those standardized newsletters that are available. Some are interested but doubt whether they are capable of doing one. But no matter what their feelings, most have no idea of how they could start writing and publishing a newsletter. If any of these descrip-tions fit you, let me encourage you. You can do a very good newsletter; but to be effective it has to be from you.

One of the solutions many advisors choose is to use one of the standardized financial newsletters that you can buy from your company, broker dealer, or outside vendor. These newsletters are usually put together in a very professional fashion. You, as the advisor, are allowed to personalize the letter by adding a picture or a name and address to the newsletter. Some allow even further customization by having a personal article from you as a possible "drop-in" feature. Others may allow you a choice of different articles to be included that are more appropriate to your clients. There are many options, and these newsletters often contain helpful financial material, insights, and information. But they have major problems when it comes to helping you market yourself in your business. First, they are not personally from you, and then, they are produced for everybody. Remember what we learned about broadcasting. If you try and reach everybody with everything, you usually reach nobody with nothing. These standardized letters are written by someone who does not know you, or anything about your business or your clientele. Like any other piece of communication they will more often than not fail due to a lack of focus, intensity, and impact.

There is another reason why these standardized newsletters are not up to performance marketing standards. Today's consumer, and your client, is pretty savvy. They understand how most of these documents and newsletters work. They can see the standardization. One advisor told me of a client who commented about one of these newsletters in a joking but pointed way "Aren't you smart enough to figure out what to say yourself?"

If you want to be more successful, you better have something to say and you better say it well. You also need to demonstrate that the reader needs you, not just information. Remember, you make the difference. You want your newsletter to reflect the wisdom, warmth, perhaps even the wit and the expertise, which comes from you and you alone.

> *"If you want to be more successful, you better have something to say and you better say it well."*

Education and information are not the goals of a good marketing newsletter

The standardized newsletters provide general educational information about financial topics. But your goal should not be just to educate your readers, but for your reader to be increasingly engaged to you as a person, not to some abstract impersonal data. You, not some anonymous writer, are to be a source of wisdom and information. Your newsletter should seek to portray you, not just as an expert professional, but as an interesting and inspiring person. In some respects, you don't want to provide or attempt to fully educate your readers. The goal is not to help them do it themselves. The goal from your marketing perspective is for them to understand the complexities of the issues involved and to realize that they cannot do it themselves. They need help; they need you.

More reasons for the newsletter to be from you

When the newsletter is from you, there are even greater marketing advantages than just demonstrating your wisdom, experience, and expertise. You can demonstrate your personality and personal style. One of my clients has a very dry sense of humor and a keen wit. His simple newsletter often features jokes and stories that bring a smile and elicit fun comments from clients, colleagues, and people who know him. The newsletter reflects well on the warmth of his personality. People find that attractive. Another client wrote in his newsletter about the death of a beloved dog and the challenge to replace him. It struck a very personal note. Many people called to comment, share similar stories, ask questions, and offer condolences. The conversations led to further reviews, appointments, recommendations, and new business. With the newsletter from you, you can advertise special events, make special offers, hold contests, and offer things of value that clients and prospects can only get from you. Your programs, seminars, offers for books and tapes, free consultations, and suggestions for further help can all be featured.

When the newsletter comes from you . . . you can focus on others

The standard newsletters are very general. They are for everybody everywhere. But when you design the newsletter, you design it for very specific people—your readers, clients, and prospects. If your practice has a strong emphasis on retirement planning, you will focus your articles and information on that part of life for your readers. But you can take it even further. You can feature stories about clients who have now retired and who are enjoying the fruits of your mutual success due to your counsel and advice. They will be flattered. Others will recognize them, and those who are featured will probably show it or forward it to their family and friends. Are you beginning to see the possibilities? You can also have stories of community interest as well as client success. If clients and friends have achieved some local recognition or received an award, mention it. In this way, others are not only interested in your newsletter, but they help in the distribution as they share it with others, because it is not only from you but also for them. Please remember those words, "from you and for them."

"Please remember those words, 'from you and for them.' "

Some objections to doing your own newsletter

There are often a number of objections raised when I suggest the "newsletter from you." The first is the issue of compliance. "How will I get this past compliance?" is a common response. That can be an issue, particularly in today's often over-regulated environment, but it need not be a great concern. Your newsletter should not be an attempt to explain complicated market, investment, or tax strategies. You should stick to simple informational concepts about your services and the things that you do. For the most part, your newsletter should be a friendly, engaging report and review of things and ideas of interest that are neither complicated nor controversial. So even though your newsletter will have to go through the compliance department of your company or broker dealer, there should be little in your newsletter that requires extensive screening. With good preparation and by following these guidelines, you can send your material to the compliance department (by e-mail), and they should be able to get it back to you in record time. It is important that you insist that your compliance colleagues give you the fastest possible turnaround time on your newsletter material. I have clients who are averaging twenty-four to forty-eight hours on turnaround time when the newsletter is well constructed. If your company or broker/dealer is much past that "real time measure," think about making some changes.

Some others object, by saying they do not have the talent to put together a newsletter. That can be overcome. You may not have the necessary writing skills, but if you are a good advisor, you must have some good ideas and communication skills. Find someone to help you or coach you. Strategic Coach Dan Sullivan has it right when he says, "Delegate everything but your genius."[3] There are writers and editors available to take some of your rough and ragged thoughts and turn them into effective and finished prose. I often suggest that clients go to a journalism department of a local college and seek a student or intern to help them put the newsletter together. You sit down with your writer editor, explain what you would like to say, and describe what you want to accomplish. The writer editor will capture your thoughts and words and put them down into polished written prose. This is perfectly legitimate and ethical. In fact, many articles and books written by celebri-

> *"Find someone to help you or coach you."*

ties, politicians, and business leaders are done this very way. It is your thoughts, and their writing.

When the newsletter is done, consult with your e-mail or Internet Service Provider to find a listserver or the best way to put all of your e-mail addresses together and combine them with your newsletter in a word processing format. Once you do have the system in place, sending your newsletter can be as simple as a few clicks. Your wisdom, warmth, and offers are sent around the world at e-speed.

There is one objection, however, that I have no answer for. From time to time, I hear someone object to a newsletter by saying, "Well, I just have nothing to say." If that is the case, and I doubt it really is, then you might want to consider another career or business. If you're going to try and make it as a financial advisor by selling products, policies, and port-folios, you are ill prepared for the future in this industry. If a client or prospect is going to benefit from your wisdom, counsel, and advice, then you need to have something to say. Today, you must be well read, well informed, and thoughtful in the work that you do. If you think about it, and if you're good at what you do, you probably have a lot to say. Remember, you make the difference and your newsletter demonstrates that with every excellent issue.

How to start doing a newsletter from you

With these ideas in hand, you can start a newsletter with these four simple steps:

Ask permission, always ask permission

The most powerful question words that you can use in marketing are: "With your permission I would like to _____." Fill in the blank with your request. In this case you say, "With your permission I would like to send you my newsletter." The words "with your permission" give great power to you and the person to whom you are speaking. You have the confidence to ask knowing that they can choose. They have the power to refuse. But when asked in this way, they seldom do. This means you only have people on your newsletter list that have given their permission. Since they have requested your newsletter, you are not a SPAMMER. It is vital that you offer your newsletter with every contact, interview, program, talk and connection; wherever there might be some interest. So call your present clients and prospects and ask permission. If a person does not want your newsletter, you've discovered something about your relationship and

> *". . . call your present clients and prospects and ask permission."*

that should be a point of thought and action for you. If they do, thank them and assure them that you will not give their name to others, nor will you overload their mailbox with useless advertising. The newsletter will contain helpful, interesting, and occasionally some just-for-fun information. Again, if they do not want your newsletter, you say, "I understand. As I said, I do this only with your permission, so nothing will be sent. Perhaps you might want to reconsider at a later time." Either way, you will discover there is great power in asking permission.

Start with one page

Many people are discouraged by the amount of information a newsletter seemingly requires. Don't be anxious about that. Make a commitment to a one to two page e-mail newsletter. Choose a title to start with. You can always change it later. Since you are starting this with e-mail, you will not want to include fancy formats or graphics. A very respectable newsletter is simple formatted titles and text. As your sophistication grows and the technology improves, you can do more. But right now, we just want to get a start.

Start by including four parts

First, have a small lead article that reflects your thoughts on money, the meaning of success, a current situation, or long-term strategy. This does not have to be a long piece—150 to 300 words are fine. This is a place to demonstrate your thoughtfulness. You don't have to have some great original idea (there are very few of those). You can comment, reflect on an idea, or pass on something you have learned. Ask yourself this question: "Does this demonstrate thoughtfulness and communicate personal warmth?"

In the second part, you can offer a simple resource. Here you might suggest a book, an article, or pamphlet that the reader might find helpful. You review or comment on the source, explain why it is helpful, and how it can be found, purchased or read. You can put in the URL of a link that takes the reader to an on-line bookseller, a Web-site, or to the actual article, story, or document itself. This should be related to your business specialty, but it does not have to be that financially specific. Remember, you are an advisor who is helping people achieve significant goals so they can enjoy life and experience true success. So you need to recommend things that are helpful for people who care about improving themselves and living well.

> *"Remember, you are an advisor who is helping people achieve significant goals so they can enjoy life and experience true success."*

Then, thirdly, have a human interest piece. This is where you demonstrate your interest in people, our world, and the community. The door is wide open. You can feature clients and their achievements. You can tell a story about people who reflect your values. You can encourage people by sharing stories of people overcoming obstacles to achieve good things. You may even have a light touch and share a funny or humorous incident. Just don't do this at someone else's expense. Always make sure that the joke is on you, not somebody else. I had one client who used this part of the newsletter to share her story of taking her oldest child to his first year of college. The calls and conversations that came from this common human-interest article lead to further and deeper relationships. It also led to more business.

Finally, and this should be your shortest part, make sure you offer a very simple description of what you do and how people can contact you. This is not to be a hyper sales piece or some ego inflated description of how good you are. It simply reminds people of who you are, what you do, and that you do it very well. Thank the reader for their attention. If they wish to unsubscribe, tell them how. Remind them that you only come into their life and work with their permission. You can also suggest that if they enjoyed it, they might want to forward it on to someone else. Think of all the possibilities.

Get a coach and get started

There are other things that you need to know about doing a newsletter, but these will get you started. Find a coach or someone with experience to help keep you moving in the direction of newsletter publications. One of my clients took the challenge seriously and discovered that he had a real gift for writing a newsletter, and it made his marketing efforts very enjoyable. Writing a good newsletter is all a part of personal performance marketing.

When the newsletter is truly from you, it will help the client understand that when it comes to financial counsel, planning, and advice that you truly make the difference. Many advisors have found that they do not need a brochure. They simply use a copy of the latest issue of their newsletter as the handout that they give to prospects. It is up-to-date, personal and friendly because it is from you and for them. But if you still think you need a brochure to go along with your tape or newsletter, we can do that too. That's next.

Chapter 12

YOU Are The Brochure When YOU Tell YOUR Story

"Your marketing efforts have to be ongoing, consistent and relentless Hi Tech. Low Tech, No Tech and sometimes totally shameless."   – Patricia Fripp

"Nothing is more practical than for people to deepen themselves. The more you understand the human condition, the more effective you are as a businessperson. Human depth makes business sense."   – Peter Koestenbaum

As we come to the final part of our guidebook to personal performance marketing, you can already sense a problem. Things are changing so fast that it's possible that many of the ideas and practices I have suggested may soon be out of date. Is that a problem? I believe that many of these ideas and instructions will be helpful and effective for some time. I am confident that some of them will stand the test of a long time because they are based on some unchanging truths about success. But many of my specific suggestions will need to be modified because of the rapid changes in the marketplace, the financial services industry, and emerging technologies. Who knows what will be possible in the next

few years in communication technology? It is already
possible to send video clips to clients and prospects by e-
mail. Because of this and other developments, some believe
that paper brochures will soon be history. We can't predict
the future but things will be different. You need to consider
these differences.

You will have to consider web-sites

The questions people ask indicate that things are changing.
You don't have to think back too far to remember when fax
machines were relatively new. Clients and prospects used to
ask, "Do you have a fax number?" They now assume you do,
and would wonder about any business that did not. The
same thing will happen with new technological and
marketing ideas. I remember the day after a presentation
when a woman asked, "What's your web-site address?" She
did not ask if I had one, she assumed that I did. Soon it will
be assumed that you have a web-site and e-mail address, as
well as a mobile phone. Maybe in the future it will be
assumed that you have a global positioning satellite address-
finder in your car. There's no telling where the technology
will lead.

In the immediate future, every advisor in the business
will need to have a web-site and a way to link to real-time
market quotes. But the actual ways of the web and how it
will work cannot even be predicted in an article, let alone in
a small guidebook like this. As soon as I would say it, it will
be out of date somewhere. Just as e-mail will grow as a way
of communicating and connecting, web-sites will be a
fundamental way of presenting ourselves, publishing our
reports, articles, books, and linking to other sources and

sites of service, information, and experience. You will simply need to keep up. You can have your company or broker-dealer help you and you need to find coaching to help you define the purpose of your web-site, design it in an attractive and user-friendly way, and find ways to attract traffic. But a company site will not be enough. Like the newsletter, it will have to have to be from you—as you make the difference.

You will have to do "point-of-the-moment marketing"

When I was teaching broadcasting to students from around the world, I used to surprise them by telling them that radio was defined as simple media. Obviously, a radio station and all it's expensive equipment is far from simple. That is not the point. Radio is simple in the production requirements; all you need is an announcer and a microphone. The message can be easily put together, and it can go out imme-diately via on-air broadcast or by tape recording. That is why we called it simple.

I remember once producing a program on tape for later airing in the day. The program had some reflections on the news of the day and spiritual development. Just as I was leaving the studio, word came across the wires of the attempted assassination on Pope John Paul II—the world held its breath. The program I had recorded just one hour ago was now out of date. To air that program and make no mention of what was happening in the world would have made listeners wonder if I was on the same planet. But there was no real problem. Due to the simplicity of radio, we could go back and produce another program that speaks to the "point of the moment." That is exactly what we did and it went very well. You have perhaps become so used to point of the moment messages, you forget how powerful they are.

> *"You have perhaps become so used to point of the moment messages, you forget how powerful they are."*

The more your marketing messages can speak to and from current situations, the more powerful and effective they are. That is why e-mail, personal performances, and web-sites with video clips will be used more and more. They can be changed and presented as quickly as I changed the program on the day of the Pope's tragic shooting. They can be modified at a moment's notice. That's why brochures seldom qualify for powerful performance marketing because they can seldom be "point of the moment."

This leads to another possibility. Many marketing professionals have suggested that the paper brochure will be less and less effective and may eventually disappear. Anyone who has gone through the time and the trouble of designing, writing, proofing, printing, and distributing a brochure knows the challenges. It is difficult to keep them relevant and current. The time and expense in putting together a paper brochure can be significant. They will be used less and less. But they have their place with the proper understanding of how they can be used. Let's see what that might be.

You are the brochure because you make the difference

Time after time, I work with financial advisors who believe that if they just had a great brochure, they would have great results. So they spend a large amount of time and energy producing a killer brochure. In some cases, these brochures have been true masterpieces and have used some of the principles of personal marketing that we have covered. Inevitably, even though the brochure is not a disappointment, the results that they get from them often are. Brochures seldom move people into action. They best serve as reminders of a pleasant conversation and a good presentation. This does not mean that brochures are useless, but their use and effectiveness should be carefully thought through before you go to press. While the broadcast audio program can demonstrate your energy, enthusiasm, and help you create emotional connections, brochures cannot do these things very well. They are useful in giving lots of information and filling in details, but they are not very effective marketing pieces for personal performance marketing. That is why I tell my clients to remember, "You are the brochure." It is how you speak your one-minute message, what you believe, how you write, how you create experiences and build relationships that makes the difference. You are the brochure, and this is better than any piece of paper that could be produced by the best graphic designer and gifted copywriter. Spend your time, money, and energy on being a better performance marketer before you spend your money on designing a better brochure. But with all this in mind and deep in your heart, you may still want to do a paper brochure. So let me show you how to do that.

> *"It is how you speak your one-minute message, what you believe, how you write, how you create experiences and build relationships that makes the difference."*

Write your story, your professional profile, and put it on a card

It is probably true that people will always want a piece of paper that they can hold on to. Even in our digital world, we have all been conditioned to have something in our hand that we can share. Because of this, a paper brochure will not disappear entirely in the near future. There are also times when you cannot give your performance or use any of the tactics and techniques that you have learned. It may also be important that people have something to remember you by. It's also helpful to have something to give people when they ask for your card or request some information. The answer to all of these dilemmas is to create a simple "story card" brochure that tells your story and can be read in less than one minute and distributed freely to people in almost every situation. Here is how to do a simple business size envelope story card.

Get a professional photograph

If you are serious about marketing yourself and your business, you will take time to get regular professional photos taken. You should have both black and white and color versions. As you receive invitations to speak, or as you write, editors and event planners will often want a picture they can use. You should not have to scramble around on those opportunities. From experience, I can tell you that such requests usually come with an "I need it right away" attached. You have to have professional photos on file that you can provide immediately. You will also want to have your picture digitally scanned and put on a digital file that you can provide via e-mail. So get a picture taken because you will put that on your professional profile, your story card.

It is important that you seek to have full rights to your picture. When a professional photographer takes a picture, they, not you, own the picture. It is their intellectual property. Even though you paid for the sitting and the product, you do not own the photo. Technically whenever you would want to reproduce the photo for a brochure or any publication, the photographer retains rights. You might owe them a royalty. So make sure you go to a photographer who will allow you to retain rights to the photo. Many photo studios understand this and will tell you that you are the owner— that is best, but make sure that you have an understanding with your photographer before you put together your picture file. Your personal profile will be more effective if you have a picture—and you will need it for lots of other good performance marketing opportunities.

How to write your story card

This is where we bring together all the work you have done. Take some of the very good ideas and insights that you now have about your business and tell your story. Write your story card that includes these four parts:

1. Who are you and what do you do?
2. What do you believe?
3. Why are you credible and trustworthy?
4. What do you hope to achieve for the client and prospect?

These are the four parts of a good professional profile story card. Now let's look at the details. Begin your story card with your name and your picture. Then do a paragraph that describes who you are and what you do. There are a variety of ways to do this. Let's go back to those "er" or "or" words that might describe what you do that we used in putting together your mission to commission statement. Revisit those words and see if you can continue to use them. Are you an advisor or an encourager, a problem solver or a solution finder? Perhaps you are a communicator or a cheerleader. So once again, and with further reflection, choose the one, two, or perhaps three that describe you best.

Actor	Caller	Conqueror
Advocator	Calculator	Cooker
Adventurer	Caregiver	Coordinator
Advisor	Caretaker	Contributor
Ambassador	Carpenter	Counselor
Analyzer	Cashier	Counter
Announcer	Catalyzer	Creator
Arranger	Catcher	Crusader
Assister	Challenger	Customer
Auditor	Character	Customizer
Author	Cheerleader	
	Chooser	Dancer
Baker	Choreographer	Dealer
Banker	Classifier	Defender
Bargainer	Cleaner	Designer
Befriender	Coacher	Describer
Beginner	Collector	Developer
Believer	Comforter	Differentiater
Bookkeeper	Commentator	Diner
Bridger	Communicator	Discipler
Broadcaster	Competitor	Discoverer
Broker	Composer	Director
Brother	Conductor	Dispatcher
Builder	Confronter	Doctor
Buyer	Connector	Dreamer

Driver

Drummer

Educator

Empowerer

Encourager

Energizer

Engager

Engineer

Enlightener

Entertainer

Entrepreneur

Examiner

Exciter

Executor

Expediter

Experimenter

Explainer

Explorer

Extractor

Facilitator

Farmer

Father

Fighter

Financier

Finisher

Fire Fighter

Fisher

Fixer

Flyer

Focuser

Follower

Forgiver

Founder

Gardener

Gatherer

Giver

Goal Setter

Go-Getter

Grace-Giver

Grandfather

Grandmother

Greeter

Grower

Guider

Harnesser

Healer

Helper

Hope-Giver

Hospitality-Giver

Hunter

Idealizer

Importer

Influencer

Informer

Innovator

Insider

Instructor

Interfacer

Interpreter

Interrogator

Intervener

Interviewer

Introducer

Inventor

Investor

Inventurer

Jockster

Joy-Maker

Joke-Teller

Jumper

Junior

Kibitzer

Kicker

Leader

Leaver

Learner

Lecturer

Lender

Lifer

Lighter

Listener

Loader

Lobbyer

Loyalty-Lover

Lover

Maker

Manager

Manufacturer

Massager

Master

Materializer

Mender

Mentor

Mercy-Giver

Messenger

Modeler

Molder

Money-Maker

Mother

Motivator
Mover
Music Maker

Negotiator
Neighbor
Networker
Newsmaker
Noise-Maker
Nurturer

Officer
Operator
Opportunity-
Maker
Opportunity-Taker
Organizer
Orchestrator
Owner
Overcomer
Overseer

Pacesetter
Painter
Parenter
Partner
Participator
Pastor
Pathfinder
Patronizer
Patternmaker
Peacemaker
Performer
Phoner
Photographer
Philosopher
Picture-Maker

Planner
Player
Policer
Politicizer
Pollster
Practitioner
Predictor
Preparer
Prescriber
Presenter
Printer
Problem Solver
Processor
Proclaimer
Producer
Programmer
Promise Keeper
Promoter
Prophesier
Protector
Provocateur
Preacher
Publicizer
Publisher
Puller
Pusher

Quality Creator
Questor
Quilter
Questioner

Racer
Rainmaker
Rambler
Rationalizer
Reader

Realist
Rebuilder
Receiver
Reconciler
Releaser
Renovator
Reporter
Reproducer
Rescuer
Researcher
Resourcer
Restorer
Retailer
Revealer
Rider
Rouser
Rower
Ruler
Runner

Salvager
Saver
Scheduler
Searcher
Seeker
Selector
Seller
Sender
Server
Sewer
Scriptwriter
Shaker
Shipper
Shopkeeper
Singer
Sister
Skipper

Solution Finder	Testifier	Volunteer
Sower	Theorizer	Voyageur
Speaker	Thinker	
Specializer	Timekeeper	Wanderer
Sportster	Tinkerer	Warder
Starter	Trainer	Warrior
Storyteller	Translator	Watcher
Supervisor	Traveler	Wayfarer
Supporter	Tutor	Welder
Synthesizer		Wisdom Seeker
Systematizer	Underwriter	Worker
	Usher	Worshipper
Tailor		Writer
Teacher	Vendor	
Team Leader	Venturer	Yearner
Team Member	Viewer	Youngster
Teller	Visioner	
Tester		

Now tell people what it is you do in ways that are compelling and clear and that follow the words that describe you. Your previous work on your mission will make this part much easier. This part should be no more than two or three sentences.

The second thing is to make a brief statement about what you believe. Again you have already done this and perhaps have done it in great detail. Perhaps one of your marketing pieces is a simple piece of paper that outlines your major beliefs as discussed in the chapter on "Do You Believe?" Now use these same ideas and insights for your story card. Write a summary of the things that you believe. Remember, you are seeking the trust and acceptance of a very significant person in helping them deal with some of the most important issues in their life. In order to earn that trust, you should have a set of beliefs that describe what you believe about life, money, success, and service. So take some time to write a summary of some of the things that you believe are important.

Third, tell why you are credible and trustworthy. Here you have the elements of your life story. This is not a time for bragging about all of your sales awards. Why should the client or prospect care that you are a good salesperson? Tell them something about your family, your education, your community service, and your experience. Tell them about the years that you have been in the business and the kinds of people you have served. Note some of your interests and some of the service that you have given to your place of worship, service organization, and your favorite charity. Show people some of the ways that you can demonstrate that you walk with integrity. You may also want to highlight your professional certifications and degrees that demonstrate your commitment to professional growth and expertise. Give substance as well as style to your credibility.

Finally, tell them what you hope to achieve for them. Here we are back to those powerful words—**"What do you want the client or prospect to feel, experience, and do, because they work with you?"** This is where all of the work of defining your personal mission should be summarized in one paragraph. Be thoughtful, and fill the following lines with all of the emotional power you can in describing how you help people, just like them, live a full, satisfying, and successful life.

> *"What do you want the client or prospect to feel, experience, and do, because they work with you?"*

These are the basic elements of a good story card or professional profile. It may take you a lot of work and some coaching in order to put it together. But when it is done well, you will have a brochure that allows people to get to know a great deal about you, why they should trust you, and what you hope to achieve as their trusted financial coach and advisor. As one wise advisor said, "You don't have anything to offer until your story and the prospect's story meet." Now let's use the story card to meet prospects and hear their story.

> *" 'You don't have anything to offer until your story and the prospect's story meet.' "*

How to use your story card brochure

There are many ways that you can use the text and the actual card. First use it as a way for your story to meet the prospect's story. The old line in the financial services industry is, "can I have twenty minutes to tell you my story and show you what I do?" A far better approach would be to say, "I would like one minute to tell you my story and spend the rest of the time hearing about you." This is exactly how you can use your story card. Before you meet with another person, you can send it to them as an introduction to yourself. When you get together, you can thank them for reading your story and then start the conversation by flipping over a copy of your story card and simply saying, "If you had a card like this, what would it say about you?"

The goal is to have them start to tell their story. People love to talk about themselves and relish any opportunity. As you get good at it, you will find that you become like a broadcast interviewer letting people tell you all kinds of things about themselves and how you can help them. As one top financial advisor said, "If you listen to people long enough, they will tell you what they want and even describe how to best sell and service them." The story card provides an ideal way to simply ask people, "If you had a card like this, what would be your story?"

You can give your story card away at every opportunity. These are simple cards that can be carried in your briefcase, in your car, any place you come and go. They fit into a standard letter-size envelope, and they easily fit into a jacket pocket. After you give a program presentation and people ask for your card, you can simply say, "would you mind if I give you my card and tell you my story?" If they give you permission, you hand it out. Every time you make a group presentation or give a talk, you can have a stack of your story cards handy for easy distribution. Whenever you gain a recommendation, you can send one out to the people you are seeking to have some contact with. After you have had a contact with a new prospect or client, you can leave your story card as a simple reminder of your time together. You can give them out to your centers of influence and ask them to distribute them freely. They turn out to be one of the most effective and least offensive ways to let people know why they should do business with you.

> *"(Your story card is) one of the most effective and least offensive ways to let people know why they should do business with you."*

You can use the text of your story on your web-site or in any e-mail communication. One of the things you will want to have on your web-site is a biography page. You use your story, and you can also attach your "bio" story to any e-mail correspondence. When you give a presentation and the person who is going to introduce you wants some information about you so that they can do an introduction, give them your story card and give them permission to say what they wish.

But the most important thing the story card does is allow people who believe in you and want to recommend you to their clients, customers, associates, and friends, to do so very easily. They can pass on your story card knowing that it tells the story and they don't have to. They just recommend. Recommendations are the best kind of marketing ever, bar none. That is where we go next.

Chapter 13

I Am **Grateful**
When You
Recommend Me
To Others

"When you cease to make a contribution, you start to die. When someone does something well, applaud. You will make two people happy." – Samuel Goldwyn

"Half of the world is on the wrong scent in the pursuit of happiness. They think it consists in having and getting and being served by others. It consists of giving and serving others." – Henry Drummond

The goal of any good marketing program is to do less and less marketing. If you are good at what you do, and if you start to become the kind of person you want for a client, and begin to do the work of a personal performance marketer as outlined it in this book, you will begin to experience greater success. You will also have a lot more fun. As you do this, you will increasingly achieve superior results for less time, energy and expense. The reason for this is very simple and yet very mysterious.

"If you become" is still the key

Our continuing theme, and the foundation of personal performance marketing, is "if you become, they will come." The more you become a person of character and an advisor of value and wisdom, you will have more and more prospects and clients come to you. I cannot fully explain this or understand it, but I have experienced it. Brian Tracy, in his many books, tapes, and programs on personal and professional success boldly speaks of the "law of attraction."[1] He believes the universe has physical and metaphysical laws that guide us, help us, or bring us down if we seek to defy them. The law of gravity is a natural law. It can be depended on to keep us from floating off into space, and if we are up in the air, it will bring us crashing down to earth. Gravity always works. In a similar way when we say, "What goes around, comes around," we are expressing a metaphysical law. We are saying that what you sow, you will reap. If you treat people like a jerk, you will have jerky things happen to you.

These laws cannot be demonstrated by physical or scientific means. They are above physics. But to Brian Tracy and others like him, including myself, these metaphysical laws and principles are just as real as the physical laws that give order and design to our life. Tracy speaks of the law of attraction to mean that people truly have an almost magnetic force that will bring people to them as they become people of quality, character, focus, and exceptional service. You will be more focused, clear, concise, and less fearful as you learn to apply these life and marketing principles. Because of this you will be more attractive, and "they will come."

But perhaps there is not as great a mystery as all of the above might imply. What will happen is that you and your services will grow both in character, performance, and reputation. People will tell others about you, and that is what you want. One of the goals of this whole endeavor is that you will do less marketing of yourself, along with the related cost in time, money, and energy, and others will do the marketing for you! It is a whole new meaning to the expression "O-P-M, other people's money". To you and your business, it means "Other People Marketing for us." That is the goal. You will be the object of other people's conversations and recommendations.

> *"One of the goals of this whole endeavor is that you will do less marketing of your-self, along with the related cost in time, money, and energy, and others will do the marketing for you!"*

Gaining referrals and recommendations

When it comes to gaining referrals, there are books, tapes, systems, and even specialized coaches for you. It is a regular industry in itself. You've been told, and rightly so, that a good referral from a good source is the best way to build your business. So it is only natural that you and everyone else would like to get better at getting better referrals. You prob-ably believe that once you can get in front of the right people in the right circumstances . . . you can sell. So like many others you probably try to learn ways to get, ask for, and even beg for referrals. As a personal performance marketer, you can do better than that. Let's talk about deserving recommendations rather than asking for referrals.

How to do better

As a communications specialist I have discovered that the language we use and the words we speak often create our reality. Unfortunately the word "beg" is descriptive of how many people present themselves. Many advisors do seem to beg for referrals. That's a big problem. If you desperately need referrals, you will not get many. There is nothing less attractive to a client or prospect than a pushy, needy, and greedy salesperson. So be careful how you appear and how you come across. Don't beg, pester or push for referrals. That leads to another related problem—the very word "referral." If you are what you claim to be, a professional financial advisor, you want more than a referral. You want a professional recommendation. Do you sense the difference? A recommendation is more than a referral, much more. Changing your language will help you to begin changing your thinking. You don't just want a referral, you want a recommendation. Make that word a part of your language rather than referral.

> *"You don't just want a referral, you want a **recommendation**."*

Let's bring these ideas together and seek to summarize a very important possible change in your thinking. You want to stop having to ask for referrals and you want to deserve recommendations. How does that happen? It's fascinating to discover that often those advisors who get the most recommendations never ask for them. But they deserve them by the way they perform. At the same time, some of the most persistent referral chasers and pests are often those who get the least recommendations. There is a psychology that needs to be understood so we can perform in more effective ways.

The big problem with all "referral systems"

As a coach and with experience in the industry, I have learned, studied, and dealt with clients who have known all of the various referral systems being used. Some of these systems vary in subtlety as to how you approach the person you are seeking a recommendation from, and some of them are straight-in-your-face pestering so you can get some names. Regardless of how they approach it, they all suffer from one profound misunderstanding about what is going on. Getting a referral or a recommendation has very little and often nothing to do with you and what you do or say. It's often not about you at all. The issue is not you, it's about your client or contact and how they want to be viewed by their friends, family, and colleagues. You may have rendered valuable service to a client. You may have been friendly, helpful, and deserving of a great recommendation. So you ask for one in the best way you know how, and often receive nothing. Why does that happen? You see, they simply may not be comfortable putting you in contact with people they know. They may not want to have one of their colleagues or friends come up to them at their place of worship, or child's sporting event, and say, "Why in the world did you give that insurance guy or that financial planner my name and number?"

The same thing is true of phone calls that would follow a recommendation. Most of us do not want a phone call from someone that we do not know. So if giving you " a name" will lead to a phone call that someone may not appreciate; they will not want to have their name attached. Remember, when people say to you, when you request a referral, "I can't think of anyone;" what they are most likely really saying is, "I don't want to give a name to you right now because the person might not want me to do it." Unfortunately, the more you pester, or push, the more people will resist and it becomes a negative experience.

If you are a sensitive and compassionate advisor, you will not want to make the referral or recommendation process unpleasant for you and the people involved. Often I find that clients are reluctant to follow the referral system they have been taught, because they know deep inside that they would not want the same thing done to them. Remember, no system will work well if either you or the client is uncomfortable. People want their business and life experiences to be pleasant, not difficult. Smart performance marketing advisors are always seeking ways to heighten the client experience in a positive way, not diminish it or make it unpleasant.

Any system that seeks to get names that makes the person being questioned feel pressured, stressed, or manipulated will be ineffective. They may even get you a negative referral. One of my clients, a financial advisor, told me that after an attempt to get a referral, the person she was talking to was so upset they went out and told five people how rude the advisor was. This person was very thoughtful and was more than a little distressed by how the referral system she had used hurt her in her small community. This leads to another psychological and personal awareness truth.

The recommendation system has to work for you

I remember the day an advisor came to me after my workshop and told me that what I had just said was an emotional and career lifesaver. It was the best news that he had ever had in any of his sales and marketing training. What was this life and career changing truth? I simply said this, "If the referral or recommendation system you have been taught to use and may be trying to use does not work for you, it does not work." It is a profound truth, one that I learned from the great sales motivator and marketer, Harvey Mackay. One of Mackay's words of wisdom in looking at business and sales systems is, "if it doesn't work for you, it doesn't work."[2] Your recommendations script, system, or strategy must be comfortable, and it must work for you.

> *"Your recommendations script, system, or strategy must be comfortable, and it must work for you."*

In too many cases in our industry, what has been done is that someone has found someone else who is good at getting referrals and taken their strategy and put it on books and tapes. These books and tapes are then distributed to the field force so that everyone in the company can learn that referral method. Does that sound familiar? Think about what that means for a moment. Each of us is very different with very different practices and very different clients. A strategy that worked for one person in La Jolla, California, may not work in Birmingham, Alabama or Freeport, Maine. What worked for one person with a strong and aggressive personality may not work for another person who finds the strength of their character rather than their personality truly attractive to their clients. One attracts by boldness, energy and speaking while the other attracts with their calmness and listening presence.

You must find a system and a strategy that works for you. It must be something that you are very comfortable in saying and doing. It must be something that suits your personality, your temperament, and your way of working with people. Any attempt to do otherwise will cause you to be reluctant in performing, and it will upset your performance. Right now, I can hear some of the old timers say, "No, Stan, you have to be willing to step out of your comfort zone and do it anyhow!" Wrong! Old myths die hard, and this industry is full of old myths. But when it comes to putting together a recommendation system for you, this myth has to die. What you need to do with your practice and experience is expand your comfort zone. When we try to perform out of our comfort zone, we become reticent, reluctant, frightened and ineffectual. The challenge is to find something that does work. That's next.

> *"What you need to do with your practice and experience is expand your comfort zone."*

Your recommendation system has to be about them and for them

Please remember this, and remember this well. The best kind of personal performance marketing is when the other person feels that the whole reason for the event they are participating in is for them. Everything is directed toward them and what they want. Let me give you an example. If any professional advisor would call me, and after making an appointment to see me, actually tells me that he was expecting me to recommend him to others before he has actually done anything for me, he has just lost my business forever. When you, as a part of your recommendation process, start talking about you and you being recommended by them to others, you are saying in effect, that the whole conversation is about what you want and what you need and not about what they want and what they are seeking.

Here's another example. Let's say that years ago when I was first dating my wife I sat down and said, "Karen, I'd like to spend the next thirty minutes talking about me!" What do you think would have happened to me? Let's make it even worse. If at the end of our evening while I was taking her back to the dormitory, I would have said, "Karen, this has been a delightful time. You know that I like girls. Perhaps you can suggest some other girls in the dormitory that I might also call upon." Many people laugh when I tell that "story" at my workshops. Then I remind them that in many cases the approach we use in our business is no different than what they are laughing at.

So my challenge is this: is your recommendation system one that truly honors and respects the other person and treats them as if they were the most important person in the world? I can tell you that if you consistently practice this in the way you work with people, they will give you recommendations, and they will give them all the time. The way a recommendation system works best is when two people are having a conversation. One of the persons expresses a concern or a need. The one who is listening relates to that, connects to that, and remembers you. They then suggest that the person call you. The person is so impressed by the passion and intensity of the recommendation, they call as recommended. Have you ever gotten a call like that? Isn't it delightful? Isn't that the way you really want to do business? The answer is obvious and it is so for an obvious reason.

When you get that kind of a recommendation, the person calling you no longer thinks of you as a salesperson but as a professional advisor. For all practical purposes, when that person makes the call to you, the sale has already been made. Isn't that usually true? So think about that, and as I used to say in broadcasting when I wanted the listener to reflect on their behavior, "just let that sit on your head for a while."

But you do want recommendations, and as we have said, the best way to get that recommendation is to deserve it. It is not when you ask for it, but when you earn it, that you will get a recommendation. Ask yourself, have you done anything exceptional and out of the ordinary? You will also get a recommendation when your clients and contacts are comfortable giving your name to others. If you haven't gotten a recommendation from a satisfied client yet, you may not be at the stage in your relationship where they are ready to give it. Keep serving, keep connecting, keep being of value, and keep performing, and soon you will deserve a recommendation.

> *"It is not when you ask for it, but when you earn it, that you will get a recommendation."*

Deserving and seeking recommendations

When do you deserve a recommendation and how can you get it? That is a good question. We mentioned another well-known coach in our industry, Dan Sullivan. I like one of Sullivan's ideas and share it often. In discussing the entrepreneurial environment, Sullivan points out that "entrepreneurialism" is difficult for most people because we have been conditioned in our culture in such a way that we have an entitlement mentality. We have been taught from our earliest days, particularly in America, that we are entitled to many things and have many rights. Dan claims we have no entitlements, and only one right. We have the right to create value.[3] He is absolutely right. You do not deserve a recommendation because you sold somebody something. You do not deserve a recommendation because you delivered a policy or put a plan together. You do not even deserve a recommendation because you gave customary and usual service. You only deserve a professional recommendation when you have created extraordinary value and given the client a delightful experience that they can receive from nobody else.

Good recommendations will only come from the quality of service and experience provided both to prospects as well as present clients. If you want a recommendation, you must perform in such an extraordinary way that the person who receives your services is profoundly helped, changed, and perhaps even transformed. You must consciously be seeking to give prospects and clients such tremendous value that they cannot get the same service and experience from anyone else. I continually coach my clients to be aware of what they are going to do with clients that could be delightful as well as helpful on each and every contact. I challenge them as I now challenge you, to go to each appointment prepared to share such wit, warmth and wisdom that you would have the perfect right to charge $200 an hour for the time together even if the client bought nothing. Start taking this challenge seriously, and you will start getting recommendations without even asking.

There may be signs for seeking recommendations

You may agree with my premise and still ask, "Are there times though when you can ask for or suggest recommendations?" Once again, you must find the script, the system, or the style that works for you. To help you, you need to know something about recommendation signs. In your sales training, you were probably taught that there are what we call "buying signs." You've probably learned what these buying signs are and you know what to do when you receive them. In marketing, there are also some signs that can lead us to seeking recommendations. You are receiving recommendation signs whenever a client or prospect makes statements likes these:

- *I wish I had done this sometime ago.*
- *My brother should have done something like this.*
- *This is really a neat idea.*
- *How do you know this!*
- *Thank you very much.*

You can begin to see where this is leading. Here a client or prospect is showing that they have been impressed and that they have been helped. Whenever a client or a prospect compliments you on the work you've done or suggests that others would be well advised to know about what you have done, that's a sign. If they express deep appreciation for the creativity and insight that you have provided to them, once again, you are receiving recommendation signs. When you begin to hear things like this, this is your cue that it might be the right time to suggest a recommendation. If something like that happens, may I suggest you do this. Put down your pen or pencil, give full attention to the person and say something like this, *"You know, that really makes me happy. One of the things I enjoy about my work is discovering that what I have done has been very helpful to people like you. You know I'd like my business to grow by working with more people like you . . . when you recommend me to others, I am very grateful."*

This may not be your exact script, but it accomplishes these things. First of all, you have given full attention to the client or prospect. Second, you have given them a compliment by telling them that you really appreciate working with people like them. Thirdly, you want your business to grow by working with people just like them. There is nothing wrong with wanting your business to grow. That is the goal of a good business. But most importantly, it allows the clients to respond as they wish. They will not feel pressured or coerced or manipulated in any way. It truly allows them to have control, feel comfortable about what you have said, and enjoy the experience. At that time, they may literally recommend that you call certain people. Great! That is what you wanted.

If that happens, there is more you can do. Thank them for that, and then suggest they call that person and recommend that they call you. When they do and that person calls, you have become what you want to be, a person who attracts the kind of clients you want. I often challenge clients with this lofty goal. The goal of your business in terms of marketing is to never make another out-going phone call to get new business. The best kind of recommendation system is when people tell others and then they call you. If you don't

> *"The best kind of recommendation system is when people tell others and then they call you."*

begin to think this way, it will never happen that way. So whatever system or idea you use, make sure you are aware of the recommending signs, and that you have a very powerful script that accomplishes the goal of getting a recommendation. What is this simple script? When someone has shown appreciation for your work simply say, "thank you and I am grateful when you recommend me to others."

The goal is to receive a lot of good recommendations and to receive them in a way that is enjoyable and helpful for you, the person who recommends you and for the one who could benefit from your services. Here are some things to remember that will help you receive better recommendations and have fun at the same time.

Learn and use the power of positioning

If you have done the work suggested you will find it easier to get recommendations. That's because of an all important marketing concept called "positioning." To get good recommendations you need to be well positioned in the mind of the clients and centers of influence that you hope will recommend you. If you take these suggestions seriously, you are going to be in "a position."

Positioning is when you make sure that you and the clientele you are working with clearly understand who you are, what you do, and the value that you can bring to them. One of the problems in our industry today is that most of the people are poorly positioned. They try and do a little bit of everything

"Positioning is when you make sure that you and the clientele you are working with clearly understand who you are, what you do, and the value that you can bring to them."

and therefore nobody can understand specifically what they do in order to justify recommending them to others. Oftentimes before you can have a good recommendation system in place, you will need to continue to do the work of deciding what business you truly are in. If you have no clear message and no clear mission, you will not receive many recommendations because people will have a hard time explaining to their friends and colleagues just what it is you do. If all that you have is a general advising practice, you will probably have to keep on selling and hope for the best when it comes to recommendations.

Positioning has also been described as owning a piece of the client's and prospect's mind. Positioning means that you come to mind. When through the promotional and performance marketing work you do, the way you touch people's lives, and the way that you communicate what you do, they fully understand you and the value that you bring. That means that in the course of every day conversations, your clients and contacts will run into people who will need what you do. If you have done the work of positioning yourself, you will come to mind. They will then be able to recommend you whenever they enter into a conversation about some of the things that you do.

Keep in mind that the best recommendations come about when people are talking about life, money, and business over the table, on the golf course, as they go about their day. A problem or situation comes up and you come to mind. That's positioning. If you are well positioned, you will soon receive professional recommendations. Most of the top performers that I work with in our industry have found out how to do this. As I often say, they don't need recommendations because they have plenty of business. They don't even

ask for them, but they get them all
the time. So you need to ask, "How
well positioned are you in your
practice, in your business, and in
the minds of your clients and
prospects?" There are other simple
ways to keep well positioned in the
minds of others. Let's note just a
few.

> " 'How well posi-
> tioned are you in
> your practice, in
> your business, and in
> the minds of your
> clients and
> prospects?' "

Saying thank you with simple gifts

As I said before, everybody is listening to an imaginary radio
station. That station is WII-FM. It stands for "What's In It—
For Me." Remember that when somebody does something
for you. It is only right, and in some cases truly practical,
that you seek to do something for them. Any recommendation that is not followed by a very nice thank you note is a
recommendation that was undeserved. I have also discovered and used in my coaching practice what we call "simple
gifts."

A simple gift is not a calendar or something that adver-
tises your business. A simple gift is a gift that says "thank
you" but requires no obligation or other expectations. One
very successful multi-line insurance advisor simply sends
two movie gift certificates along with his profound thanks
when he receives a recommendation. One financial advisor
gives a gift certificate to the clients who recommend him to
others. If a client feels the gift certificate is something that
they don't want to participate in, he then encourages them
to give it to one of their favorite charities or causes that they
believe in. One of my most successful clients looked me

straight in the eye and said, "Stan, one of the secrets of my success is the practice of gifting." I am not in a position to suggest what kind of gift you should give to your clients. That is something that you and your system and your relationships will have to decide. There are also legal and compliance issues that must be considered. Perhaps a coach, colleague, or another advisor could help you. If you wish to be successful in putting together an on-going recommendation system, you must consider the power of simple gifts.

Recommend them to others

It hardly needs to be said, but one of the best ways to receive recommendations is to give them. Do you continually recommend your clients, your friends, and the people you work with to others? Do you have sources of everything from a good dog groomer to car dealer to top-notch attorney that you can continually recommend to other people? Once again, there is a natural metaphysical law that says, "If you give, you will receive." The best way to get a recommendation is to give one.

"The best way to get a recommendation is to give one."

Yes, they will not only come, they will send their friends

We said at the beginning of this chapter, the goal of any business is to live on "Other People's Marketing." We want our clients to do all of the marketing and recommending for us. Many of you have heard of the concept called "raving fans." It describes what you want. You want people who know what you do, that you are good at what you do, and enjoy telling others about you. What we have been talking about in this chapter is a simple philosophy. It says that when you truly delight in what you do and create such an experience for people that you serve, they will talk about you. Today, we often call that "buzz." Your goal should be to be the kind of person and advisor that people buzz about. This will take time because anything of value takes time. That's how we finish up.

Chapter 14

The Marketing Rule of Seven Changes EVERYTHING

"The secret of success is constancy of purpose." – Disraeli

"Everyday do something that will inch you closer to a better tomorrow." – Doug Firebaugh

"Don't be afraid to give your best to what seemingly are small jobs. Every time you conquer one it makes you that much stronger. If you do the little jobs well, the big ones tend to take care of themselves." – Dale Carnegie

One of the most common questions I hear when I give a workshop or a coaching presentation on "You Make the Difference" and personal performance marketing for financial advisors is, "Well, how long will all this take before I finally get some great results?" It is a fair question, but it also reflects one of the problems that most advisors have when they start to think with a performance marketing perspective for their life and their business. Marketing does not promise quick results and overnight changes. In fact, it often seems to be a long and difficult way to do the work, and when the

pressure gets too high, many fall
back and just go out and try and
sell somebody something. Personal
performance marketing as we have
described it requires faith in your
expertise, your value, and even in
God at times. It requires an extra
amount of patience and persistence.

> *"Personal perform-
> ance marketing as
> we have described it
> requires faith in
> your expertise, your
> value, and even in
> God at times."*

Unfortunately, many people are not well prepared to
practice those qualities. Many of us are products of our
"right now culture." We want what we want and we want it
now. Many people don't handle adversity and delayed
success very well. I often say, in a take-off of our fast food
way of thinking about life, that "we want it our way, right
away, in the driveway." To take a marketing perspective on
your business requires patience, persistence, and a belief
and enjoyment in the value of service to others that makes
you distinct and different. It also means that you hope to
make a difference in the lives of others. It means that you
understand that these good things take time. Often I hear
people in our industry say that you have to find them, sell
them, service them, and get them to give you names. If you
have followed us this far, you understand that I am
suggesting a different way. The best way to find them is to
attract them, and the way to attract them is to serve them
first and to serve them well. It is to create experiences that
engage them. It is to speak well and serve even better than
you speak.

The personal performance marketing perspective helps
you be the difference you want to be. It helps you market
yourself with power and precision. It means you give value,

service, and a great experience to those you want to be clients of your business. You do not sell them and then service them. You service them, and then they will buy and eventually recommend you to others. Do you believe that? Do you have the patience to carry on until it begins to pay off for you in significant and fun ways? Can you fight the fear that will tend to make you into a desperate needy sales-person? Can you remain a confident poised mission-based marketer of financial services when things are not going just as you want them to?

It is that kind of purpose and poise that you will need to be a successful marketer. It is very much like any good investment. The positive and long term results you seek will only come if you avoid thinking like the day trader who simply does short-term transactions and turnover trades. You need to work for long-term service performance and attraction. Good marketing takes time, but the results are worth it. You will have a lot more fun. Clients will come, and you will know how to speak, perform, expand your influence, and gain the recommendations that will continue to make your business grow. But to continue to do that, you need to fill your mind and spirit with good ideas and keep acting on them. So here are some further insights to help you make it all come together.

First you say "thank you"

First you say, "thank you." We talked about the power of simple gifts in your recommendation system. That needs to be a part of the way you say thank you for the good words and business contacts that you receive from clients, colleagues, and centers of influence. But the most effective personal marketing script you can develop consists of the four words "Thank you very much." I often remind people of the simple words of St. Paul in the Christian scriptures. In his letters to friends and colleagues he often begins by saying, "I thank God for every remembrance of you." He is essentially saying, "I am thankful for you." Do you sense the power in that? When you say thank you to people for what they do for you, and when you say you are thankful for who they are, you've just created one of the best experiences ever. The simple thank you note, handwritten and personal, creates good will and good feelings. It positions you as grateful, courteous, and with more than just a touch of class. A simple name card that can be sent out as a postcard or in an envelope is vital to your personal performance marketing. Use it to thank people for recommendations, for renewals, for their business, and for any act of kindness. You can also thank them for the memories. The minister can be thanked for his sermon. The teachers thanked for their patience, and the doctors for their kindness. The list of possible "thank you's" is endless. Your desk should have a stack of personalized note cards that you use to say "congratulations," "how are you," "thinking of you," and "thank you."

Too often, the only time people hear from their advisor is when they want something—an appointment, a review, a sale, or a recommendation. Why not surprise people by calling or leaving a message from time to time when all you want to say is thank you. Now there is a catch, a beautiful paradox to this whole idea. You have to really mean it. This is not to be just another marketing trick. Don't say thank you so that you can have an in. Say "thank you" because you truly are thankful. I have had clients do this to their clients, and they have been amazed by the response. There is so little gratefulness and appreciation in the business environment today that people are often surprised and pleased just to hear those simple and memorable words.

Let me give you an example of something you can do, and should do, every year. On the Wednesday before Thanksgiving, block out your entire day. Go through your client list and seek to contact as many clients as you can. Whether they are available for your call or if you just connect with the voicemail, it makes no difference at all. Once you are connected, simply introduce yourself and say something like this:

> *"Tomorrow is Thanksgiving Day. I wanted to call and just let you know how thankful I am for your trust and confidence in me. I am very thankful that you have chosen to do business with me. Have a great Thanksgiving Day."*

This simple script said with heartfelt thanks is just a way to begin to develop a real attitude of gratitude. One of the best ways to fight fear in our life is to always have a spirit of gratefulness within us. This Thanksgiving Day scenario should be repeated every year and modifications of it should be found throughout the year. So remember, say thank you. Say it often, and it will continue to go well for you. But like all good things, it will take time.

"So remember, say thank you. Say it often, and it will continue to go well for you."

Make your service second to none

Unfortunately, millions of marketing dollars and marketing messages are lost in the marketplace every day due to sloppy customer service. This leads to what we call in communications theory a "mixed message." In everyday language, it simply means that your walk does not match your talk. Remember, the best marketing messages and efforts are most effective when they are matched by personal performance. One of the most effective uses of your personal energy is to market to your present clients by providing pleasurable and great experiences and profound memories. These are the people who will be the source of new prospects and clients. I am continually amazed at how many people spend money and time to woo new clients at the expense of serving the clients they already have. It is common sense that a retained client that recommends you, is preferable to extending effort finding a new person who does not know you. That is why you need to be continually performing, connecting, and creating experiences of value for people.

> *"It is common sense that a retained client that recommends you, is preferable to extending effort finding a new person who does not know you."*

Significant people expect to be serviced before the sale, during the sale, and after the sale before any recommendations are given. Make sure your marketing efforts give value-added service even before any business is done and that it grows in intensity and intimacy from then on.

In the chapter on recommendations I mentioned the mindset in which you always seek to deliver value at every opportunity. I challenge you again. Be so good in your service, your presentation, and your performance that you would have the right to request that the client or prospect write a check for $200 for information presented, advice given, and wisdom shared. Now in today's environment, you may not be able to operate that way, but you can think that way. Go into a presentation fully prepared to give at least $200 of value just in the initial interview. Be prepared to do the same thing at every service opportunity or client review. Those are the standards you need to set for yourself and then work out the details to make them a reality.

Create a standard for client service

You may not want to publish it, and you may not make it public, but every good financial advisor should give careful attention to the standards of client service that they are committed to maintaining. Write out five to seven things that you promise to do to enhance the client service experience to your present clientele. Many of these things can flow out of the things that you have already stated in your beliefs about life, business, success, and service. They may flow out of industry standards and your own expectations. As you write out these five to seven service standards, consider such things as how and when you return phone calls and e-mails. How are client inquiries to be handled? How are client complaints noted, adjusted, and handled? How are visits to your office choreographed and put together? How will you resolve any disputes that you have? How will you manage the database to maintain privacy as well as good contact information? There are other standards that may come to you as you look at yourself, the emerging standards in the industry, what your technology allows, and most importantly, how would you like to be treated if you were in the client's situation. One of the best pieces of advice that one of my clients has given to his staff is simply this: "Ask yourself what the client really wants and then do your best to help them get it."

Seek client response at every opportunity

Years ago, there was a mayor of New York City by the name of Ed Koch. He was well known for going around the streets of the city and asking, "How am I doing?" It became a little bit of a joke, and certainly all the problems of urban life were not solved. But the mere fact that he opened himself up to listening to people had a powerful impact on the people of the city. Make every opportunity to follow up on client phone calls and inquiries. It is well worth your time to simply call up and ask, "how did we do?" If you ask with sincerity and integrity, you will most likely get an honest response and probably a great deal of kindness in return. Occasionally, it might be helpful to send out a client survey, but remember that a survey is very impersonal. It may help identify some deep and angry concern that somebody has, but generally, people want the personal touch. So as a part of your client service system, have a way to continually ask the Mayor Koch Question, "How am I doing?"

> *"Make every opportunity to follow up on client phone calls and inquiries."*

Never defend yourself

One of the ways I lighten the load of people who carry a great deal of responsibility is when they have made some mistake in terms of missing an appointment time or something similar, I say "well if that's the biggest mistake you make today, you will do just fine." We all make mistakes. You will make mistakes. You will be misunderstood. When you do and when you are, what do you do? A very wise man once said, "Never defend yourself." When I queried him on this, he replied with a very simple statement. If you did no wrong, you don't need to defend yourself . . . and if you did, you shouldn't. You may explain why you did what you did, and why you took certain actions, but defending yourself and attacking others will gain you nothing. When you make a mistake, admit it, take full responsibility for it, and say, "I'm sorry. What can I do within my power to make it right for you?" This peace-making mindset will serve you well, and it is one of the best marketing views of client service that you can have.

On the other hand do not allow you or your staff to suffer abuse. I said, "never defend yourself." But this does not mean you should allow yourself or your staff to be emotionally and verbally abused. This is vital. We all make mistakes and we do everything in our power to reconcile those mistakes. But you are a professional advisor, not some street peddler who puts out shoddy goods and services. No one has the right in seeking redress to abuse other people. Certainly people can get angry and be upset. However, you need to have a clear and thoughtful position, well communicated to your staff, that there are limits to what you allow people to do. Maintain your self-respect by not allowing clients to become abusive people. It is not good for you and it is not good for them. Understand where the limits are and have a script well in place. One client service associate has a simple line when the caller crosses the line that the firm has set. She says, "I am sorry that you are upset with what happened. I can understand that, but I will not accept your talking to me in that manner. Please call back when you are less upset . . . then I will be happy to talk with you." She then politely and quietly hangs up. She reports that when she handles it this way, inevitably, people call back in a few minutes apologizing for their behavior and the reconciliation process can continue. If clients persist in abusive behavior, the relationship should be ended for your sake and for theirs. Know where client service ends and abuse begins, and don't go there.

In conclusion, remember that great client service is still the best marketing effort. It is personal performance at its most profound. I have worked with financial advisors and their firms who have not observed many of the standard rules of marketing and have taken very few of the ideas that I have suggested. Yet, their business has continued to grow (it could have grown faster if they would have done better marketing) because of the simple fact that their standards of client service were exceptional. If you do nothing else, or get nothing else from this book, take the time to make your client service a stellar performance and a great experience.

The marketing rule of seven can change your life

It is one of those simple principles, but when the understanding goes from your mind to your heart to the way you live, it can change your life, your business, and certainly your marketing practices. In many of his marketing books, Jeffrey Lant speaks of the Rule of Seven.[1] There are many variations of this rule. You may have heard about them in the so-called wave or drip marketing theories. Lant is much more helpful. The essence of his idea is that it will take seven touches before the marketing message you are delivering will have any significant impact. Lant describes how this idea was formulated during the Great Depression by the Hollywood movie industry. That was the time in which a movie was a welcome diversion from the hardships of living. However, the movie cost money and even though admission was cheap by today's standards, it could be a considerable investment for people of the time. The industry learned that getting people into the theater took a variety of approaches and that people would usually require seven "touches" before they would spend their hard earned money on the theater.

In my own work, I have modified the Rule of Seven based upon my own experience and numerous anecdotal studies and discussions with other financial service advisors. The Marketing Rule of Seven as we believe it says this; "People will only make a significant decision to work with you after seven positive touches from you." Let's look at the details. This does not mean that somebody might not buy a simple insurance policy or carry out a simple transaction after one contact or touch. It is obvious that simple non-emotional, non-significant decisions are made all the time, in every part

> *" 'People will only make a significant decision to work with you after seven positive touches from you.' "*

of the marketplace. I believe that a significant decision is one that requires a great deal of personal and financial commitment, and is only made on the average after seven favorable touches have been experienced by the prospect.

This is not the same as wave or drip marketing. Sending somebody a letter or a piece of advertising may not be a positive experience. In fact, it may be in their words, "a damn nuisance." So please don't mistake this for any theory of persistent marketing. Persistence may be a virtue, but persistence can easily become the mark of the professional pest. The seven touches must be of a positive nature; they must be things that the prospect delights in, experiences personal warmth, finds of value, and enjoys. I have challenged many financial advisors to go back and do an experience audit to think through the various "touches" that they provided to their best clients. They often discover that the first positive touch was not given by them at all, but by the person who recommended them. Obviously, another reason for providing exceptional service.

When you go through this experience audit with most of your very good clients, you will find that seven is very close to the average number of positive touches you provided before they became fully engaged to you as a close client and advocate. Obviously, in some situations, there were less than seven, and there are many in which there were over seven. The Marketing Rule of Seven needs to sit on your head and sink into your heart and become a part of your view of personal performance marketing. People come to you when they have been touched significantly, deeply, and repeatedly.

"People come to you when they have been touched significantly, deeply, and repeatedly."

This takes all of the pressure out of your first and second and third contacts with people. You fully understand that when you go to meet a new prospect, you are on touch number one, or touch number two. You are now simply trying to give more positive experiences and to enjoy being with them, getting to know them and to hear their story. You can live in the confidence that if you continue to have the opportunity to give positive experiences to enough people that the business will come to you. This makes all of your presentations more relaxed, more fun, and less oppressive. You take time to enjoy one another knowing that before anything significant will happen in terms of financial gain or opportunity, a number of good things have to happen first. Contrary to what people tell you, your job is not to go out and make appointments, close deals, and get the checks. That will happen. Your role is to go out and by demonstrating your wit, warmth, wisdom, and expertise to make as many positive touches and create as many positive experiences as you can for as many people as you can.

"Your role is to go out and by demonstrating your wit, warmth, wisdom, and expertise to make as many positive touches and create as many positive experiences as you can for as many people as you can."

This makes your newsletters, your thank you notes, your simple gifts, your presentations, your tapes, your workshops, and your seminars all the more enjoyable. The pressure is off. Instead of "always be closing," you can live in the freedom of always be connecting, always be giving value, always be creating positive experiences. When the Marketing Rule of Seven begins to rule your marketing efforts, things will go well for you.

A statement that comes from the lore and legend of the great physicist and mathematician, Albert Einstein, can summarize all of this. Einstein spent his life seeking to discover the mathematical laws and physical phenomenon that ruled the universe. But Einstein was also curious to better know the things that determine not only the state of the universe, but of our own lives and personal experiences. Einstein is said to have come to the end of his life having concluded that he knew the meaning and purpose of human life. Einstein believed that all of us are here for others; we are here to serve one another. I believe that. Do you? In time, your service to others will bring forth the fruits of true success. Sow well, serve well, and you will live well.

Chapter 15

BREAK A LEG:
A Challenge
And A Benediction

"What would you attempt to do if you knew you could not fail? – Robert Schuller

"99% of the failures come from people who have the habit of making excuses." – George Washington Carver

"Our ultimate freedom is the right and power to decide how anybody or anything outside ourselves will affect us."
– Stephen Covey

Throughout this guidebook on personal performance marketing, I have used a theater and drama model as a way of framing what you can do. Indeed, you are not to be a warrior going out to do battle for market share in some venue of violence. You are not trying to slay the enemy. We should never use war as a business metaphor. Nor are you to be an athlete going out to beat the competition and over-come the other side. The work we do is more important than any game we might play. Ask yourself, who is the enemy and who is the competition? As a personal performance marketer—think differently! You are to be a performer stepping out on the stage in front of clients and prospects, your audience, and delighting them with your performance in such a way that they want to come back time and again. So I challenge you to begin to think this way about who you are, the work you do, and how you present yourself. That leads to some further thoughts and insights.

The world of stage and theater is full of superstition. Performers, whether they are actors or baseball players, seem to thrive on rituals, many of which remain tradition long after the superstition has passed. In no place is this more true than in the world of drama. In the theater, it was considered extremely bad luck to wish an actor good luck as they were sent off from the dressing room to the stage. So in the paradox of superstition, you would do just the opposite. You would wish an actor the worst nightmare by sending them off saying, "Break a leg." Today the backstage chatter of any play or drama still resounds with affirmations and wishes for broken limbs. So in the best of dramatic traditions, may I send you off as a performance marketer with a hearty "Break a leg!" But in doing that, I want to add a few reminders that will not only bring success to you professionally, but bring you peace of mind personally.

There is no such thing as luck

"Break a leg" aside, men and women who perform at their best and achieve true success do not need good luck. No actor or performer of any merit and achievement tries to substitute "break a leg" wishes for study, practice, and hours of rehearsal. They know that a great performance comes from dedication, passion, persistent preparation, and critical review. Luck is not the issue. In this regard, there is an old proverb that says it all, "Luck?—luck favors the prepared mind." Think about that truth and what it should mean to you. I often respond to any mention of my own personal good luck with a gentle but pointed reminder that says, "Luck? No. Hard work, amazing grace, good fortune, mercy, yes. I have had all of those things, but luck has nothing to do with it."

We all must take full responsibility for our performance and for the results we achieve. Celebrate triumphs and share them with those who have helped us achieve them. Thank them for their help. But own failures and missed opportunities, take responsibility for them, and seek to learn and live better because of them. Unfortunately the world is full of people who believe that luck, the lottery, the casino, or the hot stock is the secret to success. Do not believe that for a moment. In a similar vein, do not ever believe that anybody or anything else is responsible for your success or failure; not the company, not the broker-dealer, your clients, the policies, products, fund families, or any other investment vehicle. Again, you make the difference.

> *"We all must take full responsibility for our performance and for the results we achieve."*

In short, share best wishes and affirmations often, enjoy receiving them but remember that luck has nothing to do with true success.

Learn and improve your act

Most performers plateau at a certain stage in their career, and stay there. We mentioned Peter Brook, writer and drama director. He once bemoaned his belief that most actors stop growing in their dramatic skills shortly after the age of 30. How sad, I thought, "no better after 30." I wonder if that is true of a lot of us. I meet people in our industry all the time that have stopped becoming better. They do the minimum Continuing Education requirements and no more. They make little effort to improve their skills and their knowledge. The question most often heard from these people is, "Well, what's working now?" Don't be that way. Make every effort to improve your craft and your performance, as well as increase your knowledge and wisdom. I again recall Brian Tracy, and his two-percent-a-month principle. He challenges all of us to live and learn in such a way that you and I get better at merely two percent each month. That's right, seek ways to look back and say at the end of each month, "How did I get better by at least two percent this month?" Tracy goes on to claim that just such a small incremental improvement will mean that in three years you will be 100% better. In ten years, it will mean that you will be ten times what you were as an advisor, performance marketer, and a person of exceptional wisdom and profound purpose. Ten times better in ten years is the goal. Think what that might mean for your income.

> *"Make every effort to improve your craft and your performance, as well as increase your knowledge and wisdom."*

I often challenge advisors by saying, "If you were a stock company, would you buy stock in you?" Most great companies spend significant amounts of money in research, training, and development to improve their performance and the products that they provide. Look at your income and expense ledger. How much money have you invested in your professional development, in books, tapes, college courses, and other ways to improve your performance, your presence, and increase your knowledge and wisdom? Make that commitment and make it now. May it never be said of you, "No better after 30."

Do what you love

There is a classic piece of advice that says, "Do what you love . . . and the money will follow." It is my hope that this guide will help you love your business even more by taking away some of the fear, difficulty, and drudgery involved in making your mark in the world and in the marketplace, and in marketing yourself and your business. Do what you love is sound advice. The truly great performers in any field have found a significant piece of the work they do that they love to do. Of course, you can't love everything about what you do. There are things in our work that take time and energy, and that merely help pay the bills. But exceptional performers in our industry and in every field have been able to make their work more than work. They have found ways for what they do to give meaning to their lives, and a sense of purpose to their days. It may even be a calling, a real mission that they can live for. In some ways, it may even approach what is commonly called "a vocation"—something we may have truly been born and made for. The writer Frederick Buechner describes a vocation as, "the place where your deep gladness and the world's deep hunger meet."[2] Think about that, and ask what could that definition mean to you and the work that you do.

There is an old Shaker song entitled, "Simple Gifts," that says "It's a gift to come down in the place just right."

However, your company, your broker-dealer, your managing partner, the government, or your family cannot give you that gift. The gift of being in the place just right is a gift you have to give your-self. Remember that your success is directly related in your profession to the fun you have, the passion you possess, and the performance that you bring to the clients that you serve. Do what you love, do it well . . . and success will come to you.

"Remember that your success is directly related in your profession to the fun you have, the passion you possess, and the performance that you bring to the clients that you serve."

The best have coaches

It is obviously a marketing question of mine, and it always gets a thoughtful reaction, a smile, and a degree of compre-hension and understanding. I often ask groups of people, "What do Tiger Woods and Luciano Pavarotti have in common?" That is a perplexing question. Putting a trim and talented athlete alongside a tubby and talented tenor causes one to think. The answer is fourfold.

First of all, they are the very best at what they do. Tiger, in his pursuit of triumphs and trophies in golf, and Pavarotti, in the operatic performances that he gives, truly are top-notch—the very best in their respective industries. Secondly, they love what they do. You will never be truly great at what you do unless there is a significant part of what you do that you truly love. I doubt whether these two men love the hours of practice and rehearsal, but they love to perform at their best, please the audience, and win. Thirdly, they make a lot of money at what they do. No explanation needed. They are millionaires many times over due to their consistently high performance. Fourth, they both have coaches. The best performers always have coaches. Coaching is not necessarily remedial work. It helps us find new ways of doing our work and in being better at who we are and what we do. The world class singer still has a vocal coach. One of the world's greatest golfer has many coaches who help him with various parts of his performance. The best have coaches.

Is it time for you to get a coach? Just as a marketing aside, you might use the same principle here to describe yourself as a financial advisor coach to top clients and suggest to them that even though they are successful, they could use a coach. As I say, always be performing and marketing. I am reminded how Michael Jordan so totally respected his coach, Phil Jackson, that he once said that if Phil left the Chicago Bulls, he would leave too. And that's what he did. Your success will increase exponentially as you seek mentors and coaches to help you perform at your best, so find a coach.

"Your success will increase exponentially as you seek mentors and coaches to help you perform at your best, so find a coach."

A benediction

Those are my challenges, and now a benediction. The word "benediction' is usually heard in churches and other places of worship and religious celebration. It usually means a blessing. You and I are called to be a blessing in every encounter we have with another human being. They should be better off because you and I came in to their life. But the word "benediction" has another meaning. It literally means to speak good to one another. The Latin origin of the word is "bene" which means good, and "diction" which means speak. To give a benediction is to speak well and wish the best to another. It is something we all can do and should do.

And so finally, thank you very much dear reader for your time and attention. This book has been for you. **In the years to come, may it go well with you!**

➤ Performance Notes ➤

The following are the references and resources noted and quoted in *You Make The Difference.* We call them performance notes because they are cited and noted to not only give you the footnoted information, but to in some cases to provide a brief annotation and description to help you improve your personal performance.

INTRODUCTION

1. Peters, Tom. *Reinventing Work: The Brand You 50, Fifty Ways to Transform Yourself from an "Employee" into a Brand that Shouts Distinction, Commitment, and Passion.* New York: Alfred A. Knopf, 2000.

2. Tracy, Brian. *The Psychology of Success—Ten Universal Principles for Personal Empowerment.* Chicago: Nightingale-Conant Corporation, 1991.
   Any personal development program can use the insights of Brian Tracy, a premier motivator, speaker, and thinker for the past three decades. Tracy's many tape programs, articles, and books are wide ranging and include a number of principles, indeed, Tracy calls them "laws," that lead us to professional and personal success.

CHAPTER 1

1. Crandall, Rick, PhD. *Marketing Your Services for People Who Hate to Sell.* Lincolnwood: Contemporary Books, 1996.

2. Miller, Arthur. *Death of a Salesman.* New York: Penguin Press, 1998 (Most Recent Edition).

3. Drucker, Peter. *The Practice of Management,* New York and Evanston, Harper & Row, 1954 (Original Edition, Reissued In Later Versions).

4. Goffman, Erving. *The Presentation of Self in Everyday Life.* New York: Anchor Books, 1959.

5. Pine, Joseph B., II, and Gilmore, James H. *The Experience Economy, Work is Theatre, & Every Business a Stage.* Boston: Harvard Business School Press, 1999.

6. Palmer, Parker J. *Leading From Within, Reflections on Spirituality and Leadership.* Indianapolis: Indiana Office for Campus Ministries, 1990.

CHAPTER 2

1. Ellison, Ralph. *Invisible Man.* New York: Vintage Books, 1995 (Second Edition).

2. Armstrong, Derek Lee and Yu, Kam Wai. *The Persona Principle, How to Succeed in Business With Image Marketing.* New York: Simon & Schuster, 1996.

3. Fulgham, Robert. *All I Really Need to Know I Learned in Kindergarten: Uncommon Thoughts on Common Things.* Ivy Books, Reissue Edition 1993.

4. Nightingale, Earl.

   Earl Nightingale produced thousands of radio talks and many audiotape programs during his career as a premier motivator, speaker, broadcaster, and writer on personal development. There are a number of principles and ideas that come out of the work of this 20th century renaissance man. Any tape program by Nightingale will be worthwhile and most of his programs can still be found as provided by Nightingale-Conant Corporation, Chicago, IL

CHAPTER 3

1. Covey, Stephen R. *The Seven Habits of Highly Effective People.* New York: Simon & Schuster, 1989.

CHAPTER 4

1. Putnam, Anthony O. *Marketing Your Services, a Step-by-Step Guide for Small Businesses and Professionals.* New York: John Wiley & Sons, 1990.

   Putnam's book was written in 1990. Of the many personal marketing and public relations books, this remains one of the best. I am grateful not only for this idea, but also for introducing me to thinking about personal performance marketing. It is a "must read."

CHAPTER 5

1. Buffet, Warren.

   These oft repeated ideas and themes can be found in the many collections of the wit and wisdom of Warren Buffet. Read what you can. The following are helpful:

   > *The Essays of Warren Buffet: Lessons for Corporate America*, by Warren E. Buffet and Laurence A. Cunningham. The Cunningham Group, April 2001 (First Revised Edition).

   > *The Essential Buffet: Timeless Principles for the New Economy*, by Robert G. Hagstrom and Robert G. Warren Hagstrom, New York: John Wiley & Sons, 2001.

   > *Warren Buffet Speaks—Wit and Wisdom form the World's Greatest Investor* by Janet Lowe, New York, John Wiley & Sons, 1997.

   These books and other collections, as well as a visit to the Berkshire Hathaway website www.berkshirehathaway.com will better help you understand the thinking and the principles of this master investor. There are also numerous articles in which the principles that have guided Buffet are explained.

2. Shapiro, Dr. George, Professor of History, University of Minnesota.

   Dr. Shapiro, in his long-time teaching career in the Speech Communications Department of the University of Minnesota, has been an inspiration to many. He was my graduate advisor and I'm very grateful for all that I've learned from him.

CHAPTER 7

1. Murray, Nick. *The Excellent Investment Advisor.* Nicholas Murray, 1996.

2. West, Scott, and Anthony, Mitch. *Storytelling for Financial Advisors: How Top Producers Sell.* Chicago: Dearborn Financial Publishing, Inc., 2000.

3. Herrmann, Ned. *The Whole Brain Business Book,* New York, McGraw Hill, 1996.

4. Turner, Mark., *The Literary Mind, The Origins of Thought and Language.* New York: Oxford University Press, 1996.

CHAPTER 8

1. Hustad, Stan. *"Put Down That Phone, and You're Under Arrest."* Financial Services Journal Online. October 1999. Also available at http://www.ptmgroup.com.— the web site of PTM Group, Inc.

CHAPTER 9

1. McLuhan. *Understanding Media: The Extensions of Man.* Cambridge: MIT Press, 1994 (Reprint Edition). McLuhan revolutionized communications thinking. He is known for the quality and quantity of his ideas and the controversy that has followed them. Many claim that he understood the media better than anyone before or since, and others view him as an unscholarly propagandist and self-promoter. Whatever your

opinion, he causes you to think. This classic work is one of the ways to think about the power of the media in modern society.

CHAPTER 10

1. Wilder, Thornton. *Our Town: A Play in 3 Acts.* New York: Harperperennial Library, Reprint Edition 1998.

2. Pine and Gilmore. Ibid.

3. Brook, Peter. *The Empty Space.* New York: Atheneum, 1968.

CHAPTER 11

1. Stanley, Dr. Thomas J. *Networking With the Affluent and Their Advisors, Part One and Two.* Atlanta: Audiotape Program, The Affluent Market Institute, 1993.
   Dr. Stanley has done a great deal of research into networking and marketing with the affluent market. This has led to his most recent books, *The Millionaire Next Door, The Surprising Secrets of America's Wealthy,* written with William D. Danko, Atlanta: Long Street Press, 1996; and *The Millionaire Mind,* Kansas City: Andrews McMeel Publishing, 2000.

2. Lant, Dr. Jeffrey. E-Mail El Dorado, *Everything You Need to Know to Sell More of Your Products and Services Everyday by E-mail Without Ever SPAMMING Anyone.* Cambridge: JAL Publications, 1998.

Dr. Lant is a prolific writer of many guidebooks and texts on the art of marketing. This one covers how to use e-mail in marketing goods and services. His other many publications are very useful in helping the entrepreneur and small business owner to market their business, themselves, and the goods and services that they provide.

3. Sullivan, Dan.

Sullivan is the leader of The Strategic Coach Program based in Toronto, Ontario, Canada. "The Strategic Coach Program." The theme of "delegating everything but your genius" is one of the primary principles in his personal self development coaching program.

CHAPTER 13

1. Tracy, Brian

Much of the power of Brian Tracy's work is that he repeats a number of profound themes. The concept of metaphysical laws is central to his thinking and world view.

2. Mackay, Harvey.

This is an anecdotal quote and a part of Harvey Mackay's thinking and a theme to his work. You would be well advised to read his first book *Swim With the Sharks Without Being Eaten Alive,* New York: William Morrow and Company, 1988.

From there, you can get involved with other books and tapes that this prodigious speaker, writer, and motivator entrepreneur has produced.

3. Sullivan, Dan. Ibid.

The particular quote is from an address entitled, "The Gap, an Extended Session with Dan Sullivan," given to The Million Dollar Round Table. Sullivan's themes of full responsibility and living the entrepreneurial life can be found in many of his talks, tapes, and coaching program entitled, "The Strategic Coach Program."

CHAPTER 14

1. Jeffrey Lant.

Lant, as previously mentioned, speaks often in his writings of this idea. In his premier marketing publications and reports, he continually helps us understand the concepts that flow out of personal marketing principles and of the Marketing Rule of Seven.

CHAPTER 15

1. Brook, Peter. Ibid

2. Frederick Buechner

Buechner is a prolific writer, poet, and thinker. His concept of vocation is repeated in many of his writings and is best expressed in this powerful quotation.

About the Author

Stan describes himself as "a communicator and a coach helping and inspiring people to take full responsibility for improving their personal and organizational performance and becoming the kind of person they would love to have for a client and customer."

After being challenged to fully experience the thrill of living by faith and courage, Stan Hustad resigned a good job in education where he had established a reputation as a master teacher, sold his home and most of his possessions and became a mission volunteer for an international religious broadcasting organization. He and his family lived a life of adventure and service in the Caribbean, Latin American and Europe. He learned how to be a world-class broadcaster and trained people to be great communicators. He was a working broadcaster, program manager, and a management and communications trainer. He worked with Trans World Radio did occasional commentary with Radio Netherlands, and was trained by the BBC in London.

After returning from this adventure he went back to school and received an M.A. Degree in Communications from the University of Minnesota. He serves as a college adjunct instructor in speech communications, organizational psychology, and leadership development.

Stan is the creator and President of the PTM Group, a personal and organizational performance coaching service. PTM stands for "press toward the mark.," a biblical quotation from the writings of St. Paul, where he challenges people to set high and lofty goals. He is a personal and professional performance coach to many business owners, leaders, executives, and entrepreneurs. He is the author of numerous articles on personal effectiveness and high-impact personal performance marketing. As an inspiring speaker, coach, and workshop leader, he assists men and women to take charge of their lives, pursue their hopes and dreams, achieve their goals, and make their unique mark in the world.

Stan is the husband of Karen, working in the insurance and financial services industry; the father of Amy, with a major consulting group in Boston; and Megan, living and working in the publishing world of New York City.

For more information on the wide range of resources available from Stan Hustad and the PTM Group contact us in any of the following ways.

www.ptmgroup.com
PTM Group
Box 6474
Minneapolis, MN 55406
612 729 0420
Fax 612 729 0962
E-mail: ptmark@aol.com

To Order
You Make The Difference

_____ copies of *You Make The Difference* @ $19.00 ($30.00 Canada) each _____

Add $3.25 ($5.20 Canada) shipping & handling for the first book _____

Add .50 (.80 Canada) for each additional book (to 3 books) _____

Call for shipping rates for 4 or more books _____

TOTAL AMOUNT enclosed _____

Please send book(s) to:

Name _____

Address _____ .

City _____ State _____ Zip_____

Credit Card: ❏ Visa   ❏ Mastercard

Card holder name _____

Card number _____

Expiration date _____   Phone _____

Card holder's signature _____

Please copy and mail or fax. Or, E-mail your order to our website.*

PTM Group
Box 6474
Minneapolis, MN 55406
612-729-0420
Fax 612-729-0962
E-mail ptmark@aol.com
www.ptmgroup.com

* books will be sent to you directly from the publisher.